The Power of Awareness

THE TARCHER CORNERSTONE EDITIONS

Tao Te Ching
by Lao Tzu, translated by Jonathan Star

The Essential Marcus Aurelius
Newly translated and introduced
by Jacob Needleman and John P. Piazza

Accept This Gift: Selections from A Course in Miracles
Edited by Frances Vaughan, Ph.D., and Roger Walsh, M.D., Ph.D.
Foreword by Marianne Williamson

The Kybalion
by Three Initiates

The Spiritual Emerson
Essential Works by Ralph Waldo Emerson
Introduction by Jacob Needleman

The Four Gospels
The Contemporary English Version
Foreword by Phyllis Tickle

The Hermetica: The Lost Wisdom of the Pharaohs
by Timothy Freke and Peter Gandy

Rumi: In the Arms of the Beloved
Translations by Jonathan Star

The Aquarian Gospel of Jesus the Christ
by Levi H. Dowling

Seven Years in Tibet
by Heinrich Harrer
Foreword by His Holiness the Dalai Lama

The Aquarian Conspiracy: Personal and Social Transformation in Our Time
by Marilyn Ferguson

The New Religions
by Jacob Needleman

Love's Voice: 72 Kabbalistic Haiku
by Richard Zimler

Jeremy P. Tarcher/Penguin
a member of Penguin Group (USA) Inc.
New York

The Power of Awareness

Includes *Awakened Imagination*

NEVILLE

JEREMY P. TARCHER/PENGUIN
Published by the Penguin Group
Penguin Group (USA) Inc., 375 Hudson Street, New York, New York 10014, USA • Penguin Group (Canada), 90 Eglinton Avenue East, Suite 700, Toronto, Ontario M4P 2Y3, Canada (a division of Pearson Penguin Canada Inc.) • Penguin Books Ltd, 80 Strand, London WC2R 0RL, England • Penguin Ireland, 25 St Stephen's Green, Dublin 2, Ireland (a division of Penguin Books Ltd) • Penguin Group (Australia), 707 Collins Street, Melbourne, Victoria 3008, Australia (a division of Pearson Australia Group Pty Ltd) • Penguin Books India Pvt Ltd, 11 Community Centre, Panchsheel Park, New Delhi–110 017, India • Penguin Group (NZ), 67 Apollo Drive, Rosedale, Auckland 0632, New Zealand (a division of Pearson New Zealand Ltd) • Penguin Books, Rosebank Office Park, 181 Jan Smuts Avenue, Parktown North 2193, South Africa • Penguin China, B7 Jaiming Center, 27 East Third Ring Road North, Chaoyang District, Beijing 100020, China

Penguin Books Ltd, Registered Offices: 80 Strand, London WC2R 0RL, England

The Power of Awareness was originally published in 1952.
Awakened Imagination was originally published in 1954.
First Jeremy P. Tarcher/Penguin compilation of these works published 2012

Published simultaneously in Canada

Most Tarcher/Penguin books are available at special quantity discounts for bulk purchase for sales promotions, premiums, fund-raising, and educational needs. Special books or book excerpts also can be created to fit specific needs. For details, write Penguin Group (USA) Inc. Special Markets, 375 Hudson Street, New York, NY 10014.

ISBN 978-0-399-16266-4

Printed in the United States of America

22nd Printing

Contents

The Power of Awareness

To

Arthur and his beloved Verne
whose awareness brought this
book into being.

Chapters

This book is to reveal your infinite power, against which no earthly force is of the slightest significance. It is to show you who you are, your purpose and your destiny.

Chapter One
I Am

"All things when they are admitted are made manifest by the light: for everything that is made manifest is light."

EPH. 5:13

The "light" is consciousness. Consciousness is *one*, manifesting in legions of forms or levels of consciousness. There is no one that is not *all* that is, for consciousness, though expressed in an infinite series of levels is not divisional. There is no real separation or gap in consciousness. 'I AM' cannot be divided. I may conceive myself to be a rich man, a poor man, a beggar man or a thief, but the center of my being remains the same regardless of the concept I hold of myself. At the center of manifestation there is only one 'I AM' manifesting in legions of forms or concepts of itself and 'I am that I am.'

'I AM' is the self definition of the absolute, the foundation on which everything rests. 'I AM' is the first cause-substance. 'I AM' is the self definition of God.

"I AM hath sent me unto you"

"I AM THAT I AM"

"Be still and know that I AM God."

'I AM' is a feeling of permanent awareness. The very center of consciousness is the feeling of 'I AM.' I may forget *who* I am, *where* I am, *what* I am, but I cannot forget that I AM. The awareness of *being* remains regardless of the degree of forgetfulness of who, where and what I am.

'I AM' is that which, amid unnumbered forms, is ever the same. This great discovery of cause reveals that, good or bad, man is actually the arbiter of his own fate, and that it is his concept of himself that determines the world in which he lives. In other words, if you are experiencing ill health, knowing the truth about cause, you cannot attribute the illness to anything other than to the particular arrangement of the basic cause-substance, an arrangement which is defined by your concept 'I am unwell.' This is why you are told "Let the weak man say, 'I am strong'." Joel 3.10, for by his assumption, the cause-substance—'I AM'—is rearranged and must, therefore, manifest that which its rearrangement affirms. This principle governs every aspect of your life, be it social, financial, intellectual or spiritual.

'I AM' is that reality to which, whatever happens, we must turn for an explanation of the phenomena of life. It is

'I AM's' concept of itself that determines the form and scenery of its existence. Everything depends upon its attitude towards itself; that which it will not affirm as true of itself cannot awaken in its world. That is, your concept of yourself, such as 'I am strong," "I am secure," "I am loved," determines the world in which you live. In other words, when you say 'I am a man, I am a father, I am an American,' you are not defining different 'I AMs;' you are defining different concepts or arrangements of the one cause-substance—the one 'I AM.' Even in the phenomena of nature, if the tree were articulate it would say 'I am a tree, an apple tree, a fruitful tree.'

When you know that consciousness is the one and only reality—conceiving itself to be something good, bad or indifferent, and becoming that which it conceived itself to be—you are free from the tyranny of second causes, free from the belief that there are causes outside of your own mind that can affect your life.

In the state of consciousness of the individual is found the explanation of the phenomena of life. If man's concept of himself were different, everything in his world would be different. His concept of himself being what it is, everything in his world must be as it is.

Thus it is abundantly clear that there is only *one* I AM and *you* are that I AM. And while *I AM is infinite*, you, by your concept of yourself, are displaying only a limited aspect of the infinite 'I AM.'

"Build thee more stately mansions, O my soul,
As the swift seasons roll!
Leave thy low-vaulted past!
Let each new temple, nobler than the last,
Shut thee from heaven with a dome more vast
Till thou at length art free,
Leaving thine outgrown shell by life's unresting sea!"

Chapter Two
Consciousness

It is only by a change of consciousness, by actually changing your concept of yourself that you can "build more stately mansions"—the manifestations of higher and higher concepts. (By manifesting is meant experiencing the results of these concepts in your world). It is of vital importance to understand clearly just what consciousness is.

The reason lies in the fact that *consciousness is the one and only reality, it is the first and only cause-substance of the phenomena of life*. Nothing has existence for man save through the consciousness he has of it. Therefore, it is to consciousness you must turn, for it is the only foundation on which the phenomena of life can be explained.

If we accept the idea of a first cause, it would follow that the evolution of that cause could never result in anything foreign to itself. That is, if the first cause-substance is light, all its evolutions, fruits and manifestations would remain light. The first cause-substance being consciousness, all its evolutions, fruits and phenomena must remain consciousness. All that could be observed would be a higher or lower form or variation of the same thing. In other words, if your consciousness is the only reality, it must also be the *only* substance. Consequently, what appears to you as circumstances, conditions and even material objects are really only the products of your own consciousness. Nature, then, as a thing or a complex of things external to your mind, must be rejected. You and your environment cannot be regarded as existing separately. You and your world are *one.*

Therefore, you must turn from the objective appearance of things to the *subjective center* of things, your consciousness, if you truly desire to know the cause of the phenomena of life, and how to use this knowledge to realize your fondest dreams. In the midst of the apparent contradictions, antagonisms and contrasts of your life, *there is only one principle at work*, only your consciousness operating. Difference does not consist in variety of substance, but in variety of arrangement of the same cause-substance, your consciousness.

The world moves with motiveless necessity. By this is meant that it has no motive of its own, but is under the necessity of manifesting your concept, the arrangement of your mind, and *your mind is always arranged in the image of all you believe and consent to as true.* The rich man, poor man, beggar man or thief are not different minds, but different arrangements of the same mind, in the same sense that a piece of steel when magnetized differs not in substance from its demagnetized state but in the arrangement and order of its molecules. A single electron revolving in a specified orbit constitutes the unit of magnetism. When a piece of steel or anything else is demagnetized, the revolving electrons have not stopped. Therefore, the magnetism has not gone out of existence. There is only a rearrangement of the particles, so that they produce no outside or perceptible effect. When particles are arranged at random, mixed up in all directions, the substance is said to be demagnetized; but when particles are marshalled in ranks so that a number of them face in one direction, the substance is a magnet. Magnetism is not generated; it is displayed. *Health, wealth, beauty and genius are not created; they are only manifested* by the arrangement of your mind—that is, by your concept of yourself. The importance of this in your daily life should be immediately apparent.

The basic nature of the primal cause is consciousness. Therefore, the ultimate substance of all things is *consciousness.*

Chapter Three

Power of Assumption

Man's chief delusion is his conviction that there are *causes other than his own state of consciousness.* All that befalls a man—all that is done by him—all that comes from him—happens as a result of his state of consciousness. A man's consciousness is all that he thinks and desires and loves, all that he believes is true and consents to. That is why a change of consciousness is necessary before you can change your outer world. Rain falls as a result of a change in the temperature in the higher regions of the atmosphere, so, in like manner, a change of circumstance happens as a result of a change in your state of consciousness.

> "Be ye transformed by the renewing of your mind."

To be transformed, the whole basis of your thoughts must change. But your thoughts cannot change unless you have *new ideas*, for you think from your ideas. All transformation begins with an intense, burning desire to be transformed. The first step in the 'renewing of the mind' is *desire*. You must want to be different before you can begin to change yourself. Then you must *make your future dream a present fact*. You do this by *assuming the feeling of your wish fulfilled*. By desiring to be other than what you are, you can create an ideal of the person you want to be and *assume that you are already that person*. If this assumption is persisted in until it becomes your dominant feeling, the attainment of your ideal is inevitable. The ideal you hope to achieve is always ready for an incarnation, but unless you yourself offer it human parentage it is incapable of birth. Therefore, your attitude should be one in which—having desired to express a higher state—you alone accept the task of incarnating this new and greater value of yourself.

In giving birth to your ideal you must bear in mind that the methods of mental and spiritual knowledge are entirely different. This is a point that is truly understood by probably not more than one person in a million. You know a thing mentally by looking at it from the outside, by comparing it with other things, by analyzing it and defining it; whereas you can know a thing spiritually only by becoming it. You must be the thing itself and not merely talk about it or look at it. You must be like the moth in search of his idol, the flame,

> "who spurred with true desire, plunging at once into the sacred fire, folded his wings within, till he became one colour and one substance with the flame. He only knew the flame who in it burned, and only he could tell who ne'er to tell returned."

Just as the moth in his desire to know the flame was willing to destroy himself, so must you in becoming a new person be willing to die to your present self.

You must be conscious of *being* healthy if you are to know what health is. You must be conscious of *being* secure if you are to know what security is. Therefore, to incarnate a new and greater value of yourself, you must assume that you already are what you want to be and then live by faith in this assumption—which is not yet incarnate in the body of your life—in confidence that this new value or state of consciousness will become incarnated through your absolute fidelity to the assumption that you are that which you desire to be. This is what wholeness means, what integrity means. They mean submission of the whole self to the feeling of the wish fulfilled in certainty that that new state of consciousness is the renewing of mind which transforms. There is no order in Nature corresponding to this willing submission of the self to the ideal beyond the self. Therefore, it is the height of folly to expect the incarnation of a new and greater concept of self to come about by natural evolutionary process. That which requires a state of consciousness to produce its effect obviously cannot be effected without such a state of consciousness, and in your ability to assume the feeling of a greater life, to assume a new concept of yourself, *you possess what the rest of Nature does not possess—Imagination—the instrument by which you create your world.*

Your imagination is the instrument, the means, whereby your redemption from slavery, sickness and poverty is effected. If you refuse to assume the responsibility of the incarnation of a new and higher concept of yourself, then you *reject the means, the only means, whereby your redemption—that is, the attainment of your ideal—can be effected.*

Imagination is the only redemptive power in the universe. However, your nature is such that it is optional to you whether you remain in your present concept of yourself (a hungry being longing for freedom, health and security) or choose to become the instrument of your own redemption, imagining yourself as that which you want to be, and thereby satisfying your hunger and redeeming yourself.

> "O be strong then, and brave, pure, patient and true;
> The work that is yours let no other hand do.
> For the strength for all need is faithfully given
> From the fountain within you—the Kingdom of
>   Heaven."

Chapter Four
Desire

The changes which take place in your life *as a result of your changed concept of yourself* always appear to the unenlightened to be the result, not of a change of your consciousness, but of chance, outer cause or coincidence. However, the only fate governing your life is the fate determined by your own concepts, your own assumptions; for an assumption, *though false*, if persisted in will harden into fact. The ideal you seek and hope to attain will not manifest itself, will not be realized by you, until you have imagined that you are already that ideal. There is no escape for you except by a radical psychological transformation of yourself, except by your assumption of the feeling of your wish fulfilled. Therefore, make results or accomplishments the crucial test of your ability to use your imagination.

Everything depends on your attitude towards yourself. *That which you will not affirm as true of yourself can never be realized by you* for that attitude alone is the necessary condition by which you realize your goal.

All transformation is based upon suggestion and this can work only where you lay yourself completely open to an influence. You must abandon yourself to your ideal as a woman abandons herself to love, for complete abandonment of self to it is the way to union with your ideal. You must assume the feeling of the wish fulfilled until your assumption has all the sensory vividness of reality. *You must imagine that you are already experiencing what you desire.* That is, you must assume the feeling of the fulfillment of your desire until you are possessed by it and this feeling crowds all other ideas out of your consciousness.

The man who is not prepared for the conscious plunge into the assumption of the wish fulfilled in the faith that it is the only way to the realization of his dream is not yet ready to live *consciously* by the law of assumption, although there is no doubt that he does live by the law of assumption unconsciously. But for you who accept this principle and are ready to live by consciously assuming that your wish is already fulfilled, the adventure of life begins. To reach a higher level of being, you must assume a higher concept of yourself.

If you will not imagine yourself as other than what you are, then you remain as you are,

> "for if ye believe not that I am He, ye shall die in your sins."

If you do not believe that you are He (the person you want to be) then you remain as you are. Through the faithful systematic cultivation of the feeling of the wish fulfilled, *desire becomes the promise of its own fulfillment.* The assumption of the feeling of the wish fulfilled makes the future dream a present fact.

Chapter Five

The Truth That Sets You Free

The drama of life is a psychological one in which all the conditions, circumstances and events of your life are brought to pass by your assumptions.

Since your life is determined by your assumptions you are forced to recognize the fact that you are either a slave to your assumptions or their master. To become the master of your assumptions is the key to undreamed of freedom and happiness. You can attain this mastery by deliberate conscious control of your imagination. You determine your assumptions in this way: Form a mental image, a picture of the state desired, of the person you want to be. Concentrate your attention upon the feeling that you are already that person. First, visualize the picture in your consciousness. Then *feel* yourself to be in that state as though it actually formed your surrounding world. By your imagination that which was a mere mental image is changed into a seemingly solid reality.

The great secret is a controlled imagination and a well sustained attention firmly and repeatedly focused on the object to be accomplished. It cannot be emphasized too much that, by creating an ideal within your mental sphere, by assuming that you are already that ideal, *you identify yourself with it and thereby transform yourself into its image.* This was called by the ancient teachers, "Subjection to the will of God" or "Resting in the Lord", and the only true test of "Resting in the Lord" is that all who *do* rest are inevitably transformed into the image of that in which they rest. You become according to your resigned will, and your resigned will is your concept of yourself and all that you consent to and accept as true. You, assuming the feeling of your wish fulfilled and continuing therein, take upon yourself the results of that state; not assuming the feeling of your wish fulfilled, you are ever free of the results.

When you understand the redemptive function of imagination, *you hold in your hands the key to the solution of all your problems.* Every phase of your life is made by the exercise of your imagination. Determined imagination alone is the means of your progress, of the fulfilling of your dreams. *It is the beginning and end of all creating. The great secret is a controlled imagination and a well sustained attention firmly and repeatedly focused on the feeling of the wish fulfilled until it fills the mind and crowds all other ideas out of consciousness.* What greater gifts could be given you than to be told the Truth that will set you free. *The Truth that sets you free is that you can experience in imagination what you desire to experience in reality, and by maintaining this experience in imagination your desire will become an actuality.*

You are limited only by your uncontrolled imagination and lack of attention to the feeling of your wish fulfilled. When the imagination is not controlled and the attention not steadied on the feeling of the wish fulfilled, then no amount of prayer or piety or invocation will produce the desired effect. When you can call up at will whatsoever image you please, when the forms of your imagination are as vivid to you as the forms of nature, you are master of your fate.

Visions of beauty and splendor,
Forms of a long-lost race,
Sounds and faces and voices,
From the fourth dimension of space—
And on through the universe boundless,
Our thoughts go lightning shod—
Some call it imagination,
And others call it God.

Chapter Six
Attention

"A double minded man is unstable in all his ways."

James 1:8

Attention is forceful in proportion to the narrowness of its focus, that is, when it is obsessed with a single idea or sensation. It is steadied and powerfully focused only by such an adjustment of the mind as permits you to see one thing only, for you steady the attention and increase its power by confining it. *The desire which realizes itself is always a desire upon which attention is exclusively concentrated*, for an idea is endowed with power only in proportion to the degree of attention fixed on it. Concentrated observation is the attentive attitude directed towards some specific end. The attentive attitude involves selection, for when you pay attention it signifies that you have decided to focus your attention on one object or state rather than on another.

Therefore, when you know what you want you must

deliberately focus your attention on the feeling of your wish fulfilled until that feeling fills the mind and crowds all other ideas out of consciousness.

The power of attention is the measure of your inner force. Concentrated observation of one thing shuts out other things and causes them to disappear. *The great secret of success is to focus the attention on the feeling of the wish fulfilled without permitting any distraction.* All progress depends upon an *increase* of attention. The ideas which impel you to action are those which dominate the consciousness, those which possess the attention.

> "This one thing I do, forgetting those things that are behind, I press toward the mark."

This means you, this one thing you can do, "forgetting those things that are behind." You can press toward the mark of filling your mind with the feeling of the wish fulfilled.

To the unenlightened man this will seem to be all fantasy, yet *all progress comes from those who do not take the accepted view, nor accept the world as it is.* As was stated heretofore, if you can imagine what you please, and if the forms of your thought are as vivid as the forms of nature, you are by virtue of the power of your imagination, master of your fate.

Your imagination is you yourself and the world as your imagination sees it is the real world.

When you set out to master the movements of attention, which must be done if you would successfully alter the course of observed events, it is then you realize how little control you exercise over your imagination and how much it is dominated by sensory impressions and by a drifting on the tides of idle moods.

To aid in mastering the control of your attention practice this exercise. Night after night, just before you drift off to sleep, strive to hold your attention on the activities of the day *in reverse order.* Focus your attention on the last thing you did, that is, getting *in* to bed and then move it backward in time over the events until you reach the first event of the day, getting *out* of bed. This is no easy exercise, but just as specific exercises greatly help in developing specific muscles, this will greatly help in developing the "muscle" of your attention. Your attention must be developed, controlled and concentrated in order to change your concept of yourself successfully and thereby change your future. Imagination is able to do anything *but only according to the internal direction of your attention.* If you persist night after night, sooner or later you will awaken in yourself a centre of power and become conscious of your greater self, the real you. Attention is developed by repeated exercise or habit. Through habit an action becomes easier, and so in course of time gives rise to a facility or faculty, which can then be put to higher uses.

When you attain control of the internal direction of your attention, you will no longer stand in shallow water but will launch out into the deep of life. You will walk in the assumption of the wish fulfilled as on a foundation more solid even than earth.

Chapter Seven
Attitude

Experiments recently conducted by Merle Lawrence (Princeton) and Adelbert Ames (Dartmouth) in the latter's psychology laboratory at Hanover, N. H., prove that what you see when you look at something *depends not so much on what is there as on the assumption you make when you look.* Since what we believe to be the "real" physical world is actually only an "assumptive" world, it is not surprising that these experiments prove that what appears to be solid reality is actually the result of "expectations" or "assumptions." Your assumptions determine not only what you see but also what you do, for they govern all your conscious and subconscious movements towards the fulfillment of themselves. Over a century ago this truth was stated by Emerson as follows:

> "As the world was plastic and fluid in the hands of God, so it is ever to so much of his attributes as we bring to it. To

> ignorance and sin, it is flint. They adapt themselves to it as they may, but in proportion as a man has anything in him divine, the firmament flows before him and takes his signet and form."

Your assumption is the hand of God moulding the firmament into the image of that which you assume. The assumption of the wish fulfilled is the high tide which lifts you easily off the bar of the senses where you have so long lain stranded. It lifts the mind into prophecy in the full right sense of the word; and if you have that controlled imagination and absorbed attention which it is possible to attain, you may be sure that all your assumption implies will come to pass.

When William Blake wrote,

> "What seems to be, is, to those to whom it seems to be"

he was only repeating the eternal truth,

> "there is nothing unclean of itself: but to him that esteemeth anything to be unclean, to him it is unclean."
>
> Rom. 14:14

Because there is nothing unclean *of itself* (or clean of itself) you should assume the best and think only of that which is lovely and of good report. It is not superior insight but ignorance of this law of assumption if you read into the greatness of men some littleness with which you may be familiar—or into some situation or circumstance an unfavorable conviction. *Your particular relationship to another influences your assumption with respect to that other and makes you see in him that which you do see.* If you can *change* your opinion of another, then what you now believe of him cannot be absolutely true but is only *relatively* true. The following is an actual case history illustrating how the law of assumption works:

One day a costume designer described to me her difficulties in working with a prominent theatrical producer. She was convinced that he unjustly criticized and rejected her best work and that often he was deliberately rude and unfair to her. Upon hearing her story, I explained that if she found the other rude and unfair, it was a sure sign that she, herself, was wanting and that it was not the producer, but herself that was in need of a new attitude. I told her that the power of this law of assumption and its practical application could be discovered only through experience and that only by assuming that the situation was *already* what she wanted it to be could she prove that she could bring about the change desired. Her employer was merely bearing witness, telling her by his behavior what her *concept* of him was. I suggested that it was quite probable that she was carrying on conversations with him *in her mind* which were filled with criticism and recriminations. There was no doubt but that she was mentally arguing with the producer, for others only echo that which we whisper to them in secret. I asked her if it was not true that she talked to him *mentally* and if so what those conversations were like. She confessed that every morning on her way to the theatre she told him just what she thought of him in a way she would never have dared address him in person. The intensity and force of her mental arguments with him automatically established his behavior towards her. She began to realize that all of us carry on mental conversations, but, unfortunately on most occasions these conversations are argumentative . . . that we have only to observe the passerby on the street to prove this assertion . . . that so many people are mentally engrossed in conversation and few appear to be happy about it, but the very intensity of their feeling must lead them quickly to the unpleasant incident they, themselves, have mentally created and therefore must now encounter. When she realized what she had been doing, she agreed to change her attitude and to live this law faithfully by assuming that her job was highly satisfactory and her relationship with the producer was a very happy one. To do this she agreed that before going to sleep at night, on her way to work, and at other intervals during the day she would *imagine* that he had congratulated her on her fine designs and that she, in turn, had thanked him for his praise and kindness. To her great delight she soon discovered for herself that her own attitude was the cause of all that befell her.

The behavior of her employer miraculously reversed itself. His attitude, echoing, as it had always done, that which she had assumed, now reflected her *changed* concept of him.

What she did was by the power of her imagination. Her persistent assumption influenced his behavior and determined his attitude toward her.

> With the passport of desire and on the wings of a controlled imagination she traveled into the future of her own predetermined experience.

Thus we see it is not facts, but that which we create in our imagination which shapes our lives, for most of the conflicts of the day are due to the want of a little imagination to cast the beam out of our own eye. It is the exact and literal minded who live in a fictitious world. As this designer, by her controlled imagination, started the subtle change in her employer's mind, so can we, by the control of our imagination and wisely directed feeling solve our problems.

By the intensity of her imagination and feeling the designer cast a kind of enchantment on her producer's mind and caused him to think that his generous praise originated with him. Often our most elaborate and original thoughts are determined by another.

"We should never be certain that it was not some woman treading in the wine-press who began that subtle change in men's mind, or that the passion did not begin in the mind of some shepherd boy, lighting up his eyes for a moment before it ran upon its way."

William Butler Yeats

Chapter Eight
Renunciation

"There is no coal of character so dead that it will not glow and flame if but slightly turned."

"Resist not evil."

"Whosoever shall smite thee on thy right cheek, turn to him the other also."

There is a great difference between *resisting evil and renouncing it.* When you resist evil, you give it your attention, you continue to make it real. When you renounce evil you take your attention from it and give your attention to what you want. Now is the time to control your imagination and

> "Give beauty for ashes, joy for mourning, praise for the spirit of heaviness, that they might be called trees of righteousness, the planting of the Lord that He might be glorified."

You give beauty for ashes when you concentrate your attention on things as you would like them to be rather than on things as they are. You give joy for mourning when you maintain a joyous attitude regardless of unfavorable circumstances. You give praise for the spirit of heaviness when you maintain a confident attitude instead of succumbing to despondency. In this quotation the Bible uses the word tree as a synonym for man. You become a tree of righteousness when the above mental states are a permanent part of your consciousness. You are a planting of the Lord when all your thoughts are *true* thoughts. He is "I AM" as described in Chapter One. "I AM" is glorified when your highest concept of yourself is manifested.

When you have discovered your own controlled imagination to be your saviour, your attitude will be completely altered without any diminution of religious feeling and you will say of your controlled imagination

> "Behold this vine. I found it a wild tree, whose wanton strength had swollen into irregular twigs. But I pruned the plant and it grew temperate in its vain expense of useless leaves, and knotted as you see into these clean full clusters to repay the hand that wisely wounded it."

By vine is meant your imagination which in its uncontrolled state, expends its energy in useless or destructive thoughts and feelings. But you, just as the vine is pruned by cutting away its useless branches and roots, prune your imagination *by withdrawing your attention from all unlovely and destructive ideas and concentrating on the ideal you wish to attain.* The happier more noble life you will experience will be the result of wisely pruning your own imagination. Yes, be pruned of all unlovely thoughts and feelings that you may

> "Think truly, and thy thoughts shall the world's famine feed; Speak truly, and each word of thine shall be a fruitful seed; Live truly, and thy life shall be a great and noble creed."

Chapter Nine
Preparing Your Place

"And all mine are thine, and thine are mine;"

JOHN 17:10

"Thrust in thy sickle, and reap; for the time is come for thee to reap; for the harvest of the earth is ripe."

REV. 14:15

All is yours. Do not go seeking for that which you are. Appropriate it, claim it, assume it. *Everything* depends upon your concept of yourself. That which you do not claim as true of yourself, cannot be realized by you. The promise is

> "Whosoever hath, to him it shall be given, and he shall have more abundance; but whosoever hath not, from him shall be taken away even that which he seemeth to have."

Hold fast, in your imagination, to all that is lovely and of good report for the lovely and the good are essential in your life if it is to be worthwhile. Assume it. You do this by imagining that you *already are* what you want to be—and *already have* what you want to have.

> "As a man thinketh in his heart so is he."

Be still and know that you are that which you desire to be, and you will never have to search for it.

In spite of your appearance of freedom of action, you obey, as everything else does, the law of assumption. Whatever you may think of the question of free will, the truth is *your experiences throughout your life are determined by your assumptions*—whether conscious or unconscious. An assumption *builds a bridge of incidents that lead inevitably to the fulfillment of itself.*

Man believes the future to be the natural development of the past. But the law of assumption clearly shows that this is not the case. Your assumption places you psychologically where you are not *physically*; then your senses pull you back from where you were psychologically to where you are physically. *It is these psychological forward motions that produce your physical forward motions in time.* Pre-cognition permeates all the scriptures of the world.

> "In my Father's house are many mansions; If it were not so, I would have told you. I go to prepare a place for you. And if I go and prepare a place for you, I will come again and

> receive you unto myself: that where I am, there ye may be also . . . And now I have told you before it came to pass, that, when it is come to pass ye might believe."
>
> John 14:2, 3, 29

The "I" in this quotation is your imagination which goes into the future, into one of the many mansions. Mansion is the state desired . . . telling of an event before it occurs *physically* is simply feeling yourself into the state desired until it has the tone of reality. *You go and prepare a place for yourself by imagining yourself into the feeling of your wish fulfilled.* Then, you speed from this state of the wish fulfilled—where you have not been physically—back to where you were physically a moment ago. Then, with an irresistible forward movement, you move forward across a series of events to the physical realization of your wish that where you have been in imagination, there you will be in the flesh also.

> "Unto the place from whence the rivers come, thither they return again."
>
> Eccles. 1:7

Chapter Ten
Creation

"I am God, declaring the end from the beginning, and from ancient times things that are not yet done."

Isaiah 46:10

Creation is finished. Creativeness is only a deeper receptiveness, for the entire contents of all time and all space while experienced in a time sequence actually co-exist in an infinite and eternal now. In other words, all that you ever have been or ever will be—in fact, all that mankind ever was or ever will be, exists *now*. This is what is meant by creation and the statement that creation is finished means that nothing is ever to be created, it is only to be manifested. *What is called creativeness is only becoming aware of what already is.* You simply become aware of increasing portions of that which already exists. The fact that you can never be anything that you are not already or experience anything not already existing explains the experience of having an acute feeling of having heard *before* what is being said, or having met *before* the person being met for the first time, or having seen *before*, a place or thing being seen for the first time.

The whole of creation exists in you and it is your destiny to become increasingly aware of its infinite wonders and to experience ever greater and grander portions of it.

If creation is finished, and all events are taking place now, the question that springs naturally to the mind is "what determines your time track?" That is, what determines the events which you encounter? And the answer is *your concept of yourself.* Concepts determine the route that attention follows. Here is a good test to prove this fact. Assume the feeling of your wish fulfilled and observe the route that your attention follows. You will observe that as long as you remain faithful to your assumption, so long will your attention be confronted with images clearly related to that assumption. For example; if you assume that you have a wonderful business, you will notice how *in your imagination* your attention is focused on incident after incident relating to that assumption. Friends congratulate you, tell you how lucky you are. Others are envious and critical. From there your attention goes to larger offices, bigger bank balances and many other similarly related events. Persistence in this assumption will result in *actually experiencing in fact that which you assumed.*

The same is true regarding any concept. If your concept

of yourself is that you are a failure you would encounter in your imagination a whole series of incidents in conformance to that concept.

Thus it is clearly seen how you, by your concept of yourself, determine your present, that is, the particular portion of creation which you now experience, and your future, that is, the particular portion of creation which you will experience.

Chapter Eleven
Interference

You are free to choose the concept you will accept of yourself. Therefore, you possess the power of *intervention*, the power which enables you to *alter the course of your future.* The process of rising from your present concept to a higher concept of yourself is the means of all true progress. The higher concept is waiting for you to incarnate it in the world of experience.

> "Now unto Him that is able to do exceeding abundantly above all that we ask or think, according to the power that worketh in us. Unto him be glory."
>
> Eph. 3:20

Him, that is able to do more than you can ask or think, is *your imagination*, and the *power that worketh in us* is *your attention*. Understanding imagination to be HIM that is able to do all that you ask and attention to be the power by which you create your world, you can now build your ideal world. Imagine yourself to be the ideal you dream of and desire. Remain attentive to this imagined state and as fast as you completely feel that you are already this ideal it will manifest itself as *reality* in your world.

> "He was in the world, and the world was made by him and the world knew him not."

> "The mystery hid from the ages; Christ in you, the hope of glory."

The "He", in the first of these quotations, is your imagination. As previously explained, there is only one substance. This substance is consciousness. It is your imagination which forms this substance into concepts, which concepts are then manifested as conditions, circumstances and physical objects. *Thus imagination made your world*. This supreme truth with but few exceptions, man is not conscious of.

The mystery, *Christ in you*, referred to in the second quotation, is your imagination, by which your world is molded. The hope of glory is your awareness of the ability to rise perpetually to higher levels.

Christ is not to be found in history nor in external forms.

You find Christ only when you become aware of the fact that *your imagination* is the only redemptive power. When this is discovered, the "towers of dogma will have heard the trumpets of Truth, and, like the walls of Jericho, crumble to dust."

Chapter Twelve
Subjective Control

Your imagination is able to do all that you ask *in proportion to the degree of your attention*. All progress, all fulfillment of desire, depend upon the control and concentration of your attention. Attention may be either attracted from without or directed from within. Attention is attracted from without when you are consciously occupied with the external impressions of the immediate present. The very lines of this page are attracting your attention from without. Your attention is directed from within when you deliberately choose what you will be preoccupied with mentally. It is obvious that in the objective world your attention is not only attracted by but is constantly *directed* to external impressions. But, your control in the *subjective state* is almost non-existent, for in this state attention is usually the servant and not the master—the passenger and not the navigator—of your world. There is an enormous difference between attention directed objectively and attention directed subjectively, and the *capacity to change your future depends on the latter.* When you are able to control the movements of your attention in the subjective world you can modify or alter your life as you please. But this control cannot be achieved if you allow your attention to be attracted constantly from without. Each day, set yourself the task of deliberately withdrawing your attention from the objective world and of focusing it *subjectively.* In other words, concentrate on those thoughts or moods which you deliberately determine. Then those things that now restrict you will fade and drop away. The day you achieve control of the movements of your attention in the subjective world, you are master of your fate.

You will no longer accept the dominance of outside conditions or circumstances. You will not accept life on the basis of the world without. Having achieved control of the movements of your attention, and having discovered the mystery hid from the ages, that *Christ in you is your imagination*, you will assert the supremacy of *imagination* and put all things in subjection to it.

Chapter Thirteen
Acceptance

"Man's Perceptions are not bounded by organs of Perception: he perceives more than sense (though ever so acute) can discover."

However much you seem to be living in a material world, *you are actually living in a world of imagination*. The outer, physical events of life are the fruit of forgotten blossom-times—results of previous and usually forgotten states of consciousness. They are the ends running true to oftimes forgotten imaginative origins.

Whenever you become completely absorbed in an emotional state you are at that moment assuming the feeling of the state fulfilled. If persisted in, whatsoever you are intensely emotional about you will experience in your world. These periods of absorption, of concentrated attention, are the beginnings of the things you harvest. It is in such moments that you are exercising your creative power—the only creative power there is. At the end of these periods, or moments of absorption, you speed from these imaginative states (where you have *not been* physically) to where you were physically an instant ago. In these periods the imagined state is so real that when you return to the objective world and find that it is not the same as the imagined state, it is an actual shock. You have seen something in imagination with such vividness that you now wonder whether the evidence of your senses can now be believed and like Keats you ask,

> "was it a vision or a waking dream?
> Fled is that music . . . Do I wake or sleep?"

This shock reverses your time sense. By this is meant that *instead of your experience resulting from your past, it now becomes the result of being in imagination where you have not yet been physically*. In effect, this moves you across a bridge of incident to the physical realization of your imagined state. The man who at will can assume whatever state he pleases has found the keys to the Kingdom of Heaven. The keys are *desire, imagination and a steadily focused attention on the feeling of the wish fulfilled.* To such a man any undesirable objective fact is no longer a reality and the ardent wish no longer a dream.

> "Prove me now herewith, saith the Lord of hosts, if I will not open you the windows of heaven, and pour you out a blessing, that there shall not be room enough to receive it."
>
> Malachi 3:10

The windows of heaven may not be opened and the treasures seized by a strong will, but they open of themselves and present their treasures as a free gift —a gift that comes when absorption reaches such a degree that it results in a feeling of complete acceptance. The passage from your present state to the feeling of your wish fulfilled is not across a gap. There is continuity between the so-called real and unreal. To cross from one state to the other, you simply extend your feelers, trust your touch and enter fully into the spirit of what you are doing.

> "Not by might nor by power but by my spirit, saith the Lord of hosts."

Assume the spirit, the feeling of the wish fulfilled, and you will have opened the windows to receive the blessing. To assume a state is to get into the spirit of it. Your triumphs will be a surprise only to those who did not know your hidden passage from the state of longing to the assumption of the wish fulfilled.

The Lord of hosts will not respond to your wish until you have assumed the feeling of already being what you want to be, for *acceptance is the channel of His action*. Acceptance is the Lord of hosts in action.

Chapter Fourteen
The Effortless Way

The principal of 'Least Action' governs everything in physics from the path of a planet to the path of a pulse of light. Least Action is the minimum of energy, multiplied by the minimum of time. Therefore, in moving from your present state to the state desired, you must use the minimum of energy and take the shortest possible time. Your journey from one state of consciousness to another, is a psychological one, so, to make the journey you must employ the psychological equivalent of 'Least Action' and the psychological equivalent is mere assumption.

The day you fully realize the power of assumption, you discover that it works in complete conformity with this principle. It works by means of attention, minus effort. Thus, with least action through an assumption you hurry without haste and reach your goal without effort.

Because creation is finished, *what you desire already exists.*

It is excluded from view because you can see only the contents of your own consciousness. It is the function of an assumption to call back the excluded view and restore full vision. *It is not the world but your assumptions that change.* An assumption brings the invisible into sight. It is nothing more nor less than seeing with the eye of God, i.e., imagination.

> "For the Lord seeth not as a man seeth, for man looketh on the outward appearance, but the Lord looketh on the heart."

The heart is the primary organ of sense, hence the first cause of experience. When you look "on the heart" you are looking at your assumptions: assumptions determine your experience. Watch your assumption with all diligence for out of it are the issues of life. Assumptions have the power of objective realization. Every event in the visible world is the result of an assumption or idea in the unseen world.

The present moment is all important, for it is only in the present moment that our assumptions can be controlled. The future must become the present in your mind if you would wisely operate the law of assumption. The future becomes the present when you imagine that you already are what you will be when your assumption is fulfilled. Be still (least action) and know that you are that which you desire to be. The end of longing should be Being. Translate your dream into

Being. Perpetual construction of future states without the consciousness of already being them, that is, picturing your desire without actually assuming the feeling of the wish fulfilled, is the fallacy and mirage of mankind.

It is simply futile day-dreaming.

Chapter Fifteen
The Crown of the Mysteries

The assumption of the wish fulfilled is the ship that carries you over the unknown seas to the fulfillment of your dream. *The assumption is everything; realization is subconscious and effortless.*

> "Assume a virtue if you have it not."

Act on the assumption that you already possess that which you sought.

> "blessed is she that believed; for there shall be a performance of those things which were told her from the Lord."

As the Immaculate Conception is the foundation of the Christian mysteries, so the Assumption is their crown. Psychologically the Immaculate Conception means the *birth of an idea* in your own consciousness unaided by another. For instance, when you have a specific wish or hunger or longing it is an immaculate conception in the sense that no physical person or thing plants it in your mind. It is self-conceived. Every man is the Mary of the Immaculate Conception and birth to his idea must give. The Assumption is the crown of the mysteries because it is the highest use of consciousness. When in imagination you assume the feeling of the wish fulfilled, *you are mentally lifted up to a higher level.* When, through your persistence, this assumption becomes actual fact, you automatically find yourself on a higher level (that is, you have achieved your desire) in your objective world. Your assumption guides all your conscious and subconscious movements towards its suggested end so inevitably that it *actually dictates the events.*

The drama of life is a psychological one and the whole of it is written and produced by *your assumptions.*

Learn the art of assumption for only in this way can you create your own happiness.

Chapter Sixteen

Personal Impotence

Self-surrender is essential and by that is meant the confession of personal impotence.

"I can of mine own self do nothing."

Since creation is finished it is impossible to *force* anything into being. The example of magnetism previously given is a good illustration. You cannot make magnetism, it can only be displayed. You cannot make the *law* of magnetism. If you want to build a magnet you can do so only by conforming to the law of magnetism. In other words, you surrender yourself or yield to the law. In like manner when you use the faculty of assumption you are *conforming* to a law just as real as the law governing magnetism. *You can neither create nor change the law of assumption*. It is in this respect that you are impotent. You can only yield or conform, and since all of your experiences are the result of your assumptions, (consciously or unconsciously) the value of consciously using the power of assumption surely must be obvious.

Willingly identify yourself with that which you most desire, knowing that it will find expression through you. Yield to the feeling of the wish fulfilled and be consumed as its victim, then rise as the prophet of *the law of assumption*.

Chapter Seventeen
All Things Are Possible

It is of great significance that the truth of the principles outlined in this book have been proven time and again by the personal experiences of the Author. Throughout the past twenty-five years he has applied these principles and proved them successful in innumerable instances. He attributes to an unwavering assumption of his wish already being fulfilled every success that he has achieved. He was confident that by these fixed assumptions his desires were predestined to be fulfilled. Time and again he assumed the feeling of his wish fulfilled and continued in his assumption until that which he desired was completely realized.

Live your life in a sublime spirit of confidence and determination; disregard appearances, conditions, in fact all evidence of your senses that deny the fulfillment of your desire. Rest in the assumption that you are already what you want to be, for in that determined assumption you and your Infinite Being are merged in creative unity, *and with your Infinite Being (God) all things are possible.* God never fails.

> "For who can stay His hand or say unto Him, 'what doest thou'?"

Through the mastery of your assumptions you are in very truth enabled to *master life*. It is thus that the ladder of life is ascended: thus the ideal is realized. The clue to the real purpose of life is to surrender yourself to your ideal with such awareness of its *reality* that you begin to live the life of the ideal and no longer your own life as it was prior to this surrender.

> "He calleth things that are not seen as though they were, and the unseen becomes seen."

Each assumption has its corresponding world. If you are truly observant you will notice the power of your assumptions to change circumstances which appear wholly immutable.

You, by your conscious assumptions determine the nature of the world in which you live. Ignore the present state and assume the wish fulfilled. Claim it; *it will respond.* The law of assumption is the means by which the fulfillment of your desires may be realized. Every moment of your life, *consciously or unconsciously*, you are assuming a feeling. You can no more avoid assuming a feeling than you can avoid eating and drinking. All you can do is control the nature of your assumptions.

Thus it is clearly seen that the control of your assumption is the key you now hold to an ever expanding, happier, more noble life.

Chapter Eighteen

Be Ye Doers

"Be ye doers of the word and not hearers only, deceiving your own selves. For if any be a hearer of the word, and not a doer, he is like unto a man beholding his natural face in a glass and goeth his way, and straightway forgetteth what manner of man he was. But whoso looketh into the perfect law of liberty, and continue therein, he being not a forgetful hearer but a doer of the work, this man shall be blessed in his deed."

JAMES 1:22-25

The word in this quotation means idea, concept or desire. You deceive yourself by "hearing only" when you expect your desire to be fulfilled through mere wishful thinking. Your desire is what you want to be and looking at yourself "in a glass" is *seeing yourself in imagination as that person.* Forgetting "what manner of man" you are is *failing to persist in your assumption.* The "perfect law of liberty" is the law which makes possible liberation from limitation, that is, the law of assumption. To continue in the perfect law of liberty is to persist in the assumption that your desire is already fulfilled.

You are not a "forgetful hearer" when you keep the feeling of your wish fulfilled constantly alive in your consciousness. This makes you a "doer of the work" and you are blessed in your deed by the inevitable realization of your desire.

You must be *doers* of the law of assumption, for without application the most profound understanding will not produce any desired result.

Frequent reiteration and repetition of important basic truths runs through these pages. Where the law of assumption is concerned—the law that sets man free—this is a good thing. It should be made clear again and again even at the risk of repetition. The real truth seeker will welcome this aid in concentrating his attention upon the *law which sets him free.*

The parable of the Master's condemnation of the servant who neglected to use the talent given him is clear and unmistakable. Having discovered within yourself the key to the Treasure House, you should be like the good servant who by wise use multiplied by many times the talents entrusted to him. *The talent entrusted to you is the power to consciously determine your assumption.* The talent not used, like the limb not exercised, withers and finally atrophies.

What you must strive after is *being.* In order to do, it is necessary to be. *The end of yearning is to be.* Your concept of yourself can only be driven out of consciousness by *another* concept of yourself. By creating an ideal in your mind, you can identify yourself with it until you become one and the same with the ideal, thereby transforming yourself into it.

The dynamic prevails over the static; the active over the passive. One who is a doer is magnetic and therefore infinitely more creative than any who merely hear. Be among the doers.

Chapter Nineteen
Essentials

The essential points in the successful use of the law of assumption are these: First, and above all, *yearning, longing, intense burning desire.* With all your heart you must want to be different from what you are. Intense, burning desire *is* the mainspring of action, the beginning of all successful ventures. In every great passion desire is concentrated.

> "As the heart panteth after the water brooks, so panteth my soul after Thee, O God."

> "Blessed are they that hunger and thirst after righteousness for they shall be filled."

Here the soul is interpreted as the sum total of all you believe, think, feel and accept as true; in other words, your present level of awareness. God means I AM, the source and fulfillment of all desire. This quotation describes how your present level of awareness longs to transcend itself. *Righteousness is the consciousness of already being what you want to be.*

Second, *cultivate physical immobility*, a physical incapacity not unlike the state described by Keats in his 'Ode to a Nightingale'.

> "A drowsy numbness pains my senses, as though of hemlock I had drunk."

It is a state akin to sleep, but one in which you are still in control of the direction of attention. You must learn to induce this state at will, but experience has taught that it is more easily induced after a substantial meal, or when you wake in the morning feeling very loath to arise. Then you are naturally disposed to enter this state. The value of physical immobility shows itself in the accumulation of mental force which absolute stillness brings with it. It increases your power of concentration.

> "Be still and know that I am God."

In fact, the greater energies of the mind seldom break forth save when the body is stilled and the door of the senses closed to the objective world.

The third and last thing to do is to *experience in your*

imagination what you would experience in reality had you achieved your goal. Imagine that you possess a quality or something you desire which hitherto has not been yours. Surrender yourself completely to this feeling until your whole being is possessed by it. This state differs from reverie in this respect: it is the result of a *controlled imagination and a steadied concentrated attention*, whereas reverie is the result of an uncontrolled imagination—usually just a day-dream. In the controlled state, a minimum of effort suffices to keep your consciousness filled with the feeling of the wish fulfilled. The physical and mental immobility of this state is a powerful aid to voluntary attention and a major factor of minimum effort.

The application of these three points:

1. Desire
2. Physical immobility
3. The assumption of the wish already fulfilled.

is the way to at-one-ment or *union with your objective.*

One of the most prevalent misunderstandings is that this law works only for those having a devout or a religious objective. This is a fallacy. It works just as impersonally as the law of electricity works. It can be used for greedy, selfish purposes as well as noble ones. But it should always be borne in mind that ignoble thoughts and actions inevitably result in unhappy consequences.

Chapter Twenty
Righteousness

In the preceding chapter righteousness was defined as the *consciousness of already being what you want to be.* This is the true psychological meaning and obviously does not refer to adherence to moral codes, civil law or religious precepts. You cannot attach too much importance to being righteous. In fact, the entire Bible is permeated with admonition and exhortations on this subject.

> "Break off thy sins by righteousness."
>
> Dan. 4:27

> "My righteousness I hold fast, and will not let it go: my heart shall not reproach me so long as I live."
>
> Job 27:6

> "My righteousness shall answer for me in time to come."
>
> Genesis 30:33

Very often the words "sin" and "righteousness" are used in the same quotation. This is a logical contrast of opposites and becomes enormously significant in the light of the psychological meaning of righteousness and the psychological meaning of sin. Sin means *to miss the mark.* Not to attain your desire, not to be the person you want to be is sinning. Righteousness is the consciousness of already being what you want to be. It is a changeless educative law that effects must follow causes. Only by righteousness can you be saved from sinning.

There is a widespread misunderstanding as to what it means to be "saved from sin". The following example will suffice to demonstrate this misunderstanding and to establish the truth. A person living in abject poverty may believe that by means of some religious or philosophical activity he can be "saved from sin" and his life improved as a result. If, however, he continues to live in the same state of poverty it is obvious that what he believed was not the truth, and, in fact, he was not "saved". On the other hand he can be saved by *righteousness.* The successful use of the law of assumption would have the inevitable result of an actual change in his life. He would no longer live in poverty. He would no longer miss the mark. He would be *saved from sin.*

> "Except your righteousness shall exceed the righteousness of the scribes and Pharisees, ye shall in no wise enter into the kingdom of heaven."
>
> Matt. 5:20

Scribes and Pharisees mean those who are influenced and governed by the outer appearances—the rules and customs of the society in which they live, the vain desire to be thought well of by other men. Unless this state of mind is exceeded, your life will be one of limitation—of failure to attain your desires—of missing the mark—of sin. This righteousness is exceeded by *true righteousness* which is always the consciousness of *already being* that which you want to be.

One of the greatest pitfalls in attempting to use the law of assumption is focusing your attention on *things*, on a new home, a better job, a bigger bank balance. This is not the righteousness without which you "die in your sins." Righteousness is not the *thing* itself; *it is the consciousness, the feeling of already being the person you want to be, of already having the thing you desire.*

> "Seek ye first the kingdom of God, and his righteousness; and all these things shall be added unto you."
>
> Matthew 6:33

The kingdom (entire creation) of God (your I AM) is within you. Righteousness is the awareness that you *already* possess it all.

Chapter Twenty-one

Free Will

The question is often asked, "what should be done between the assumption of the wish fulfilled and its realization?" *Nothing.* It is a delusion that, other than assuming the feeling of the wish fulfilled you can do anything to aid the realization of your desire. You think that you can do something, you want to do something; but, actually you can do nothing. *The illusion of the free will to do is but ignorance of the law of assumption* upon which all action is based. Everything happens automatically. All that befalls you, all that is done by you—*happens.* Your assumptions, *conscious or unconscious,* direct all thought and action to their fulfillment. To understand the law of assumption, to be convinced of its truth, means getting rid of all the illusions about free will to act. Free will actually means *freedom to select any idea you desire.* By assuming the idea *already* to be a fact, it is converted into reality. Beyond that, *free will ends* and everything happens in harmony with the concept assumed.

"I can of mine ownself do nothing . . . because
I seek not mine own will, but the will of the
Father which hath sent me."

In this quotation the Father obviously refers to God. In an earlier chapter, God is defined as I AM. Since creation is finished, the Father is never in a position of saying *"I will be."* In other words, everything exists and the infinite I AM consciousness can speak only in the *present tense.*

"Not my will but thine be done."

"I will be" is a confession that *"I am not"*. The Father's will is *always* "I AM". Until you realize that YOU are the Father (there is only one I AM and your infinite self is that I AM) your will is always *"I will be."*

In the law of assumption your *consciousness of being* is the Father's will. The mere wish without this consciousness is the "my will". This great quotation, so little understood, is a perfect statement of the law of assumption.

It is impossible to *do* anything. You must *be* in order to do.

If you had a different concept of yourself, everything

would be different. You are *what you are*, so everything *is as it is*. The events which you observe are determined by the concept you have of yourself. If you change your concept of yourself, the events ahead of you in time are altered, but, thus altered, they *form again a deterministic sequence* starting from the moment of this changed concept. You are a being with powers of intervention, which enable you, by a change of consciousness, to alter the course of observed events—in fact, to *change your future*.

Deny the evidence of the senses, and assume the feeling of the wish fulfilled. Inasmuch as your assumption is *creative* and forms an atmosphere, your assumption, if it be a noble one, increases your assurance and helps you to reach a higher level of being. If, on the other hand, your assumption be an unlovely one, it hinders you and makes your downward way swifter. Just as the lovely assumptions create a harmonious atmosphere, so the hard and bitter feelings create a hard and bitter atmosphere.

> "Whatsoever things are pure, just, lovely, of good report, think on these things."

This means to make your assumptions the highest, noblest, happiest concepts. There is no better time to start than *now*. The present moment is always the most opportune in which to eliminate all unlovely assumptions and to concentrate only on the good. As well as yourself, claim for others their Divine inheritance. See only their good and the good in them. Stir the highest in others to confidence and self-assertion, by your sincere assumption of their good and you will be their prophet and their healer, for an inevitable fulfillment awaits all sustained assumptions.

You win by assumption what you can never win by force. An assumption is a certain motion of consciousness. This motion, like all motion, exercises an influence on the surrounding substance causing it to take the shape of, echo, and reflect the assumption. A change of fortune is a new direction and outlook, merely a change in arrangement of the same mind substance—*consciousness.*

If you would change your life, you must begin at the very source *with your own basic concept of self.* Outer change, becoming part of organizations, political bodies, religious bodies, is not enough. The cause goes deeper. The essential change must take place *in yourself,* in your own concept of self. You must assume that you are what you want to be and continue therein, for the *reality of your assumption has its being in complete independence of objective fact,* and will clothe itself in flesh if you persist in the feeling of the wish fulfilled. When you know that assumptions, if persisted in, harden into facts, then events which seem to the uninitiated mere accidents will be understood by you to be the logical and inevitable *effects* of your assumption.

The important thing to bear in mind is that you have *infinite free will in choosing your assumptions*, but no power to determine conditions and events. *You can create nothing, but your assumption determines what portion of creation you will experience.*

Chapter Twenty-two
Persistence

"And He said unto them, Which of you shall have a friend, and shall go unto him at midnight, and say unto him, Friend, lend me three loaves; for a friend of mine in his journey is come to me, and I have nothing to set before him? and he from within shall answer and say, Trouble me not: the door is now shut, and my children are with me in bed; I cannot rise and give thee. I say unto you, Though he will not rise and give him, because he is his friend, yet because of his importunity he will rise and give him as many as he needeth. And I say unto you, Ask, and it shall be given you; seek, and ye shall find; knock, and it shall be opened unto you."

LUKE 11:5-9

There are three principle characters in this quotation; you and the two friends mentioned. The first friend is a *desired state of consciousness*. The second friend is a *desire seeking fulfillment*. Three is the symbol of wholeness, completion. Loaves symbolize substance. The shut door symbolizes the senses which separate the seen from the unseen. Children in bed means ideas that are dormant. Inability to rise means a desired state of consciousness cannot rise to you, you must rise to it. Importunity means demanding persistency, a kind of brazen impudence. *Ask, seek* and *knock mean assuming the consciousness of already having what you desire.*

Thus the scriptures tell you that you must persist in rising to (assuming) the consciousness of your wish already being fulfilled. The promise is definite that if you are shameless in your impudence in assuming that you *already have* that which your senses deny, it shall be given unto you—*your desire shall be attained.*

The Bible teaches the necessity of persistence by the use of many stories. When Jacob sought a blessing from the Angel with whom he wrestled, he said

> "I will not let thee go, except thou bless me."

When the Shunammite sought the help of Elisha, she said,

> "As the Lord liveth, and as thy soul liveth, I will not leave thee, and he arose and followed her."

The same idea is expressed in another passage.

> "And he spake a parable unto them that men ought always to pray, and not to faint; saying, There was in a city a judge, which feared not God, neither regarded man, and there was a widow in that city; and she came unto him, saying Avenge me of mine adversary. And he would not for a while; but afterward he said within himself, Though I fear not God, nor regard man; yet because this widow troubleth me, I will avenge her, lest she weary me by her continual coming."
>
> Luke 18:1-5

The basic truth underlying each of these stories is that desire springs from the awareness of ultimate attainment and that persistence in maintaining the consciousness of the desire already being fulfilled results in its fulfillment.

It is not enough to feel yourself into the state of the answered prayer; you must persist in that state. That is the reason for the injunction

> 'man ought always to pray and not to faint';

here, *to pray means to give thanks for already having what you desire.* Only persistency in the assumption of the wish fulfilled can cause those subtle changes in your mind which result in the desired change in your life. It matters not whether they be "Angels", "Elisha" or "reluctant judges"; all *must* respond in harmony with your persistent assumption. When it appears that people other than yourself in your world do not act toward you as you would like, it is not due to reluctance on their part but a lack of *persistence* in your assumption of your life already being as you want it to be. Your assumption to be effective cannot be a single isolated act; it must be a maintained attitude of the wish fulfilled.

Chapter Twenty-three
Case Histories

It will be extremely helpful at this point to cite a number of specific examples of the successful application of this law. *Actual case histories are given.* In each of these the problem is clearly defined and the way imagination was used to attain the required state of consciousness is fully described. In each of these instances the author of this book was either personally concerned or was told the facts by the person involved.

1.

This is a story with every detail of which I am personally familiar.

In the spring of 1943 a recently drafted soldier was stationed in a large army camp in Louisiana. He was intensely eager to get out of the army but only in an entirely honorable way.

The only way he could do this was to apply for a discharge. The application then required the approval of his commanding officer to become effective. Based on army regulations, the decision of the commanding officer was final and could not be appealed. The soldier, following all the necessary procedure applied for a discharge. Within four hours his application was returned—marked "disapproved." Convinced he could not appeal the decision to any higher authority, military or civilian, he turned within to his own consciousness, determined to rely on the law of assumption.

The soldier realized that his consciousness was the only reality, that his particular state of consciousness determined the events he would encounter.

That night, in the interval between getting into bed and falling asleep, he concentrated on consciously using the law of assumption. *In imagination* he felt himself to be in his own apartment in New York City. He visualized his apartment, that is, in his mind's eye he actually saw his own apartment, mentally picturing each one of the familiar rooms with all the furnishings vividly real.

With this picture clearly visualized, and lying flat on his back, he completely relaxed physically. In this way he induced a state bordering on sleep at the same time retaining control of the direction of his attention. When his body was completely immobilized, he *assumed* that he was in his own room and felt himself to be lying in his own bed—a very different feeling from that of lying on an army cot. In imagination he rose from the bed, walked from room to room touching various pieces of furniture. He then went to the window and with his hands resting on the sill looked out on the street on which his apartment faced. *So vivid was all this in his imagination* that he saw in detail the pavement, the railings, the trees and the familiar red brick of the building on the opposite side of the street. He then returned to his bed and felt himself drifting off to sleep. He knew that it was most important in the successful use of this law that at the actual point of falling asleep his consciousness be filled with the assumption that he was already what he wanted to be. All that he did in imagination was based on the assumption that he was no longer in the army. Night after night the soldier enacted this drama. Night after night in imagination he felt himself, honorably discharged, back in his home seeing all the familiar surroundings and falling asleep in his own bed. This continued for eight nights. For eight days his *objective* experience continued to be directly opposite to his *subjective* experience in consciousness each night, before going to sleep. On the *ninth day* orders came through from Battalion headquarters for the soldier to fill out a new application for his discharge. Shortly after this was done he was ordered to report to the Colonel's office. During the discussion the Colonel asked him if he was still desirous of getting out of the army. Upon receiving an affirmative reply the Colonel said that he personally disagreed and while he had strong objections to approving of the discharge, he had decided to overlook these objections and to approve it. Within a few hours the application was approved and the soldier, now a civilian, was on a train bound for home.

2.

This is a striking story of an extremely successful business man demonstrating the power of imagination and the law of assumption. I know this family intimately and all the details were told to me by the son described herein.

The story begins when he was twenty years old. He was next to the oldest in a large family of nine brothers and one sister. The father was one of the partners in a small merchandising business. In his eighteenth year the brother referred to in this story left the country in which they lived and traveled two thousand miles to enter college and complete his education. Shortly after his first year in college he was called home because of a tragic event in connection with his father's business. Through the machinations of his associates, the father was not only forced out of his business, but was the object of false accusations impugning his character and integrity. At the same time he was deprived of his rightful share in the equity of the business. The result was he found himself largely discredited and almost penniless. It was under these circumstances that the son was called home from college.

He returned, his heart filled with one great resolution. He was determined that he would become outstandingly successful in business. The first thing he and his father did was to use the little money they had to start their own business. They rented a small store on a side street not far from the large business of which the father had been one of the principal owners. There they started a business bent upon real service to the community. It was shortly after that the son with instinctive awareness that it was bound to work, deliberately used imagination to attain an almost fantastic objective.

Every day on the way to and from work he passed the building of his father's former business—the biggest business of its kind in the country. It was one of the largest buildings with the most prominent location in the heart of the city. On the outside of the building was a huge sign on which the name of the firm was painted in large bold letters. Day after day as he passed by a great dream took shape in the son's mind. He thought of how wonderful it would be if it was his family that had this great building—his family that owned and operated this great business.

One day as he stood gazing at the building, *in his imagination* he saw a completely different name on the huge sign across the entrance. Now the large letters spelled out *his fam-*

ily name (in these case histories actual names are not used. For the sake of clarity in this story we will use hypothetical names and assume that the son's family name was Lordard) where the sign read F. N. Moth & Co., *in imagination* he actually saw the name letter by letter, J. N. Lordard & Sons. He remained looking at the sign with his eyes wide open *imagining* that it read J. N. Lordard & Sons. Twice a day, week after week, month after month for two years he saw his family name over the front of that building. He was convinced that if he *felt strongly enough* that a thing was true it was bound to be the case, and by *seeing in imagination* his family name on the sign—which implied that they owned the business—he became convinced that one day they *would* own it.

During this period he told only one person what he was doing. He confided in his mother who with loving concern tried to discourage him in order to protect him from what might be a great disappointment. Despite this he persisted day after day. *Two years later the large company failed and the coveted building was up for sale*. On the day of the sale he seemed no nearer ownership than he had been two years before when he began to apply the law of assumption. During this period they had worked hard, and their customers had implicit confidence in them. However, they had not earned anything like the amount of money required for the purchase of the property. Nor did they have any source from which they could borrow the necessary capital. Making even more remote their chance of getting it was the fact that this was regarded as the most desirable property in the city and a number of wealthy business people were prepared to buy it. *On the actual day of the sale, to their complete surprise, a man, almost a total stranger, came into their shop and offered to buy the property for them.* (Due to some unusual conditions involved in this transaction the son's family could not even make a bid for the property.) They thought the man was joking. However, this was not the case. The man explained that he had watched them for some time, admired their ability, believed in their integrity and that supplying the capital for them to go into business on a large scale was an extremely sound investment for him. *That very day the property was theirs.* What the son had persisted in seeing in his imagination was now a reality. The hunch of the stranger was more than justified. Today this family owns not only the particular business referred to but owns many of the largest industries in the country in which they live.

The son, *seeing his family name over the entrance of this great building, long before it was actually there, was using exactly the technique that produces results. By assuming the feeling that he already had what he desired—by making this a vivid reality in his imagination—by determined persistence, regardless of appearance or circumstance, he inevitably caused his dream to become a reality.*

3.

This is the story of a very unexpected result of an interview with a lady who came to consult me.

One afternoon a young grandmother, a business woman in New York, came to see me. She brought along her nine year old grandson who was visiting her from his home in Pennsylvania. In response to her questions, I explained the law of assumption describing in detail the procedure to be followed in attaining an objective. The boy sat quietly, apparently absorbed in a small toy truck while I explained to the grandmother the method of assuming the state of consciousness that would be hers were her desire already fulfilled. I told her the story of the soldier in camp who each night fell asleep, imagining himself to be in his own bed in his own home.

When the boy and his grandmother were leaving he looked up at me with great excitement and said, "I know what I want and, now, I know how to get it." Surprised, I asked him what it was he wanted; he told me he had his heart set on a puppy. To this the grandmother vigorously protested, telling the boy that it had been made clear repeatedly that he could not have a dog under any circumstances. . . . that his father and mother would not allow it, that the boy was too young to care for it properly and furthermore the father had a deep dislike for dogs—he actually hated to have one around.

All these were arguments the boy passionately desirous of having a dog, refused to understand. "Now I know what to do," he said. "Every night just as I am going off to sleep I am going to pretend that I have a dog and we are going for a walk." "No," said the grandmother, "that is not what Mr. Neville means. This was not meant for you. You cannot have a dog."

Approximately six weeks later the grandmother told me, what was to her, an astonishing story. The boy's desire to own a dog was so intense that he had absorbed all that I had told his grandmother of how to attain one's desire—and he believed implicitly that at last he knew how to get a dog.

Putting this belief into practice, *for many nights the boy imagined a dog was lying in his bed beside him. In imagination he petted the dog actually feeling its fur.* Things like playing with the dog and taking it for a walk filled his mind.

Within a few weeks it happened. A newspaper in the city in which the boy lived, organized a special program in connection with Kindness to Animals week. All school children were requested to write an essay on "Why I Would Like to Own a Dog."

After entries from all the schools were submitted and judged, the winner of the contest was announced. The very same boy who weeks before in my apartment in New York had told me "Now I know how to get a dog" was the winner.

In an elaborate ceremony, which was publicized with stories and pictures in the newspaper, the boy was awarded a beautiful *collie* puppy.

In relating this story the grandmother told me that if the boy had been given the money with which to buy a dog, the parents would have refused to do so and would have used it to buy a bond for the boy or put it in the savings bank for him. Furthermore, if someone had made the boy a gift of a dog, they would have refused it or given it away. But the dramatic manner in which the boy got the dog, the way he won the city-wide contest, the stories and pictures in the newspaper, the pride of achievement and joy of the boy himself all combined to bring about a change of heart in the parents, and they found themselves doing that which they never conceived possible—they allowed him to keep the dog.

All this the grandmother explained to me, and she concluded by saying that there was one particular kind of dog on which the boy had set his heart. *It was a Collie.*

4.

This was told by the Aunt in the story to the entire audience at the conclusion of one of my lectures.

During the question period following my lecture on the law of assumption, a lady who had attended many lectures and had had personal consultation with me on a number of occasions, rose and asked permission to tell a story illustrating how she had successfully used the law.

She said that upon returning home from the lecture the week before, she had found her niece distressed and terribly upset. The husband of the niece, who was an officer in the Army Air Force stationed in Atlantic City, had just been ordered, along with the rest of his unit, to active duty in Europe. She tearfully told her Aunt that the reason she was upset was that she had been hoping her husband would be assigned to Florida as an Instructor. They both loved Florida and were anxious to be stationed there and not to be separated. Upon hearing this story the aunt stated that there was only one thing to do and that was to apply immediately the law of assumption. "Let's actualize it," she said. "If you were actually in Florida, what would you do? You would feel the warm breeze. You would smell the salt air. You would feel your toes sinking down into the sand. Well, let's do all that right now."

They took off their shoes and turning out the lights, *in imagination they felt themselves actually in Florida feeling the warm breeze, smelling the sea air, pushing their toes into the sand.*

Forty-eight hours later the husband received a change of orders. His new instructions were to report immediately to Florida as an Air Force Instructor. Five days later his wife was on a train to join him. While the Aunt, in order to help her niece to attain her desire, joined in with the niece in assuming the state of consciousness required, *she* did not go to Florida. That was not her desire. On the other hand, that was the *intense longing* of the niece.

5.

This case is especially interesting because of the short interval of time between the application of this law of assumption and its visible manifestation.

A very prominent woman came to me in deep concern. She maintained a lovely city apartment and a large country home; but because the many demands made upon her were greater than her modest income, it was absolutely essential that she rent her apartment if she and her family were to spend the summer at their country home.

In previous years the apartment had been rented without difficulty early in the spring, but the day she came to me the rental season for summer sublets was over. The apartment had been in the hands of the best real estate agents for months, but no one had been interested even in coming to see it.

When she had described her predicament I explained how the law of assumption could be brought to bear on solving her problem. I suggested that by imagining the apartment had been rented by a person desiring immediate occupancy and by assuming that this was the case, her apartment actually would be rented. In order to create the necessary feeling of naturalness—the feeling that it was already a fact that her apartment was rented, I suggested that she drift off into sleep that very night imagining herself, *not in her apartment*, but in whatever place she would sleep were the apartment suddenly rented. She quickly grasped the idea and said that in such a situation she would sleep in her country home even though it were not yet opened for the summer.

This interview took place on Thursday. At nine o'clock the following Saturday morning she phoned me from her home in the country—excited and happy. She told me that on Thursday night *she had fallen asleep actually imagining and feeling that she was sleeping in her other bed in her country home many miles away from the city apartment she was occupying.* On Friday, the very next day, a highly desirable tenant, one who met all her requirements as a responsible person, not only rented the apartment but rented it on the condition that he could move in that very day.

6.

Only the most complete and intense use of the law of assumption could have produced such results in this extreme situation.

Four years ago a friend of our family asked that I talk with his twenty-eight year old son who was not expected to live.

He was suffering from a rare heart disease. This disease resulted in a disintegration of the organ. Long and costly medical care had been of no avail. Doctors held out no hope for recovery. For a long time the son had been confined to his bed. His body had shrunk to almost a skeleton, and he could talk and breathe only with great difficulty. His wife and two small children were home when I called and his wife was present throughout our discussion.

I started by telling him that there was only one solution to any problem and that solution was a change of attitude. Since talking exhausted him, I asked him to nod in agreement if he understood clearly what I said. This he agreed to do. I described the facts underlying the law of consciousness—in fact that consciousness was the only reality. I told him that the way to change any condition was to change his state of consciousness concerning it. As a specific aid in helping him to assume the feeling of already being well, I suggested that in *imagination, he see the doctor's face expressing incredulous amazement in finding him recovered, contrary to all reason, from the last stages of an incurable disease, that he see him double checking in his examination and hear him saying over and over, "It's a miracle—it's a miracle."*

He not only understood all this clearly but he believed it implicitly. He promised that he would faithfully follow this procedure. His wife who had been listening intently assured me that she, too, would diligently use the law of assumption and her imagination in the same way as her husband. The following day I sailed for New York—all this taking place during a winter vacation in the tropics.

Several months later I received a letter saying the son had made a miraculous recovery. On my next visit I met him in person. He was in perfect health, actively engaged in business and thoroughly enjoying the many social activities of his friends and family.

He told me that from the day I left he never had any doubt that "it" would work. He described how he had faithfully followed the suggestion I had made to him and *day after day had lived completely in the assumption of already being well and strong.*

Now, four years after his recovery, he is convinced that the only reason he is here today is due to his successful use of the law of assumption.

7.

This story illustrates the successful use of the law by a New York business executive.

In the fall of 1950 an executive of one of New York's prominent banks discussed with me a serious problem with which he was confronted. He told me that the outlook for his personal progress and advancement was very dim. Having reached middle age and feeling that a marked improvement in position and income was justified, he had "talked it out" with his superiors. They frankly told him that any major improvement was impossible and intimated that if he was dissatisfied he could seek another job. This, of course, only increased his uneasiness. In our talk he explained that he had no great desire for really big money but that he had to have a substantial income in order to maintain his home comfortably and to provide for the education of his children in good preparatory schools and colleges. This he found impossible on his present income. The refusal of the bank to assure him of any advancement in the near future resulted in a feeling of discontent and an intense desire to secure a better position with considerably more money. He confided in me that the kind of job he would like better than anything in the world was one in which he managed the investment funds of a large institution such as a foundation or great university.

In explaining the law of assumption, I stated that his present situation was only a manifestation of his concept of himself, and declared that if he wanted to change the circumstances in which he found himself, he could do so by changing his concept of himself. In order to bring about this change of consciousness, and thereby a change in his situation, I asked him to follow this procedure every night just before he fell asleep. *In imagination he was to feel that he was retiring at the end of one of the most important and successful days of his life. He was to imagine that he had actually closed a deal that very day to join the kind of organization he yearned to be with and in exactly the capacity he wanted.* I suggested to him that if he succeeded in completely filling his mind with this feeling, he would experience a definite sense of relief. In this mood his uneasiness and discontent would be a thing of the past. He would feel the contentment that comes with the fulfillment of desire. I wound up by assuring him that if he did this faithfully he would inevitably get the kind of position he wanted.

This was the first week of December. *Night after night without exception he followed this procedure.* Early in February a director of one of the wealthiest foundations in the world asked this executive if he would be interested in joining the foundation in an executive capacity handling investments. After some brief discussion he accepted.

Today at a substantially higher income and with the assurance of steady progress, this man is in a position far exceeding all that he had hoped for.

8.

The man and wife in this story have attended my lectures for a number of years. It is an interesting illustration of the conscious use of this law by two people concentrating on the same objective at one time.

This man and wife were an exceptionally devoted couple. Their life was completely happy and entirely free from any problems or frustrations.

For sometime they had planned to move into a larger apartment. The more they thought about it the more they realized that what they had their hearts set on was a beautiful penthouse. In discussing it together the husband explained that he wanted one with a huge window looking out on a magnificent view. The wife said she would like to have one side of the walls mirrored from top to bottom. They both wanted to have a wood-burning fire place. It was a 'must' that the apartment be in New York City.

For months they had searched for just such an apartment in vain. In fact, the situation in the city was such that the securing of any kind of apartment was almost an impossibility. They were so scarce that not only were there waiting lists for them but all sorts of special deals including premiums, the buying of furniture, etc., were involved. New apartments were being leased long before they were completed, many being rented from the blue prints of the building.

Early in the spring after months of fruitless seeking, they finally located one which they seriously considered. It was a penthouse apartment in a building just being completed on upper Fifth Avenue facing Central Park. It had one serious drawback. Being a new building it was not subject to rent control and the couple felt the yearly rental was exorbitant. In fact, it was several thousand dollars a year more than they had considered paying. During the spring months of March and April they continued looking at various penthouses throughout the city but they always came back to this one.

Finally they decided to increase the amount they would pay substantially and made a proposition which the agent for the building agreed to forward to the owners for consideration.

It was at this point, without discussing it with each other, each determined to apply the law of assumption. It was not until later that each learned what the other had done. *Night after night, they both fell asleep in imagination in the apartment they were considering. The husband, lying with his eyes closed, would imagine that his bedroom windows were overlooking the park. He would imagine going to the window the first thing in the morning and enjoying the view. He felt himself sitting on the terrace overlooking the park, having cocktails with his wife and friends, all thoroughly enjoying it. He filled his mind with actually feeling himself in the penthouse and on the terrace. During all this time, unknown to him, his wife was doing the same thing.*

Several weeks went by without any decision on the part of the owners but they continued to imagine as they fell asleep each night that they were actually sleeping in the penthouse.

One day, to their complete surprise, one of the employees in the apartment building in which they lived told them that the penthouse there was vacant. They were astonished because theirs was one of the most desirable buildings in the city with a perfect location right on Central Park. They knew there was a long waiting list of people trying to get an apartment in their building. The fact that a penthouse had unexpectedly become available was kept quiet by the management because they were not in a position to consider any applicants for it. Upon learning that it was vacant this couple immediately made a request that it be rented to them, only to be told that this was impossible. The fact was that not only were there several people on a waiting list for a penthouse in the building but it was actually promised to one family. Despite this the couple had a series of meetings with the management, at the conclusion of which the apartment was theirs.

The building being subject to rent control their rental was just about what they had planned to pay when they first started looking for a penthouse. The location, the apartment itself, and the large terrace surrounding it on the South, West and North was beyond all their expectations—and in the living room on one *side is a giant window 15 feet by 8 feet with a magnificent view of Central Park; one wall is mirrored from floor to ceiling and there is a wood-burning fireplace.*

Chapter Twenty-four
Failure

This book would not be complete without some discussion of *failure* in the attempted use of the law of assumption. It is entirely possible that you either have had or will have a number of failures in this respect—many of them in really important matters. If, having read this book, having a thorough knowledge of the application and working of the law of assumption, you faithfully apply it in an effort to attain some intense desire and fail, what is the reason? If to the question, did you persist enough?, you can answer yes—and still the attainment of your desire was not realized, what is the reason for failure?

The answer to this is the most important factor in the successful use of the law of assumption. *The time it takes your assumption to become fact, your desire to be fulfilled, is directly proportionate to the naturalness of your feeling of already being what you want to be—of already having what you desire.*

The fact that it does not feel *natural* to you to be what you imagine yourself to be is *the secret of your failure.* Regardless of your desire, regardless of how faithfully and intelligently you follow the law if you do not feel *natural* about what you want to be *you will not be it.* If it does not feel natural to you to get a better job you will not get a better job. The whole principle is vividly expressed by the Bible phrase "you die in your sins"—you do not transcend from your present level to the state desired.

How can this feeling of naturalness be achieved? The secret lies in one word—*imagination.* For example, this is a very simple illustration. Assume that you are securely chained to a large heavy iron bench. You could not possibly run, in fact you could not even walk. In these circumstances it would not be natural for you to run. You could not even *feel* that it was natural for you to run. But you could easily *imagine* yourself running. In that instant, while your consciousness is filled with your *imagined* running, you have forgotten that you are bound. In *imagination* your running was completely natural.

The essential feeling of naturalness can be achieved by *persistently filling your consciousness with imagination*—imagining yourself being what you want to be or having what you desire.

Progress can spring only from your imagination, from your desire to transcend your present level. What you truly and literally *must* feel is that *with your imagination, all things are possible.* You must realize that changes are not caused by caprice, but by a change of consciousness. You may fail to achieve or sustain the particular state of consciousness necessary to produce the effect you desire. But, once you know that consciousness is the only reality and is the sole creator of your particular world and have burnt this truth into your whole being, then you know that success or failure is entirely in your own hands. Whether or not you are disciplined enough to sustain the required state of consciousness in specific instances has no bearing on the truth of the law itself—that an assumption, if persisted in, will harden into fact. The certainty of the truth of this law must remain despite great disappointment and tragedy—even when you "see the light of life go out and all the world go on as though it were still day." You must not believe that because your assumption failed to materialize, the truth that assumptions do materialize is a lie. If your assumptions are not fulfilled it is because of some error or weakness in your consciousness. However, these errors and weaknesses *can be overcome.* Therefore, press on to the attainment of ever higher levels by feeling that you *already are* the person you want to be. And remember that the time it takes your assumption to become reality is *proportionate to the naturalness of being it.*

> "Man surrounds himself with the true image of himself. Every spirit builds itself a house and beyond its house a world, and beyond its world a heaven. Know then that the

world exists for you. For you the phenomenon is perfect. What we are, that only can we see. All that Adam had, all that Caesar could, you have and can do. Adam called his house, heaven and earth. Caesar called his house, Rome; you perhaps call yours a cobbler's trade; a hundred acres of land, or a scholar's garret. Yet line for line and point for point, your dominion is as great as theirs, though without fine name. Build therefore your own world. As fast as you conform your life to the pure idea in your mind, that will unfold its great proportion."

Emerson

Chapter Twenty-five
Faith

"A miracle is the name given, by those who have no faith, to the works of faith."

"Faith is the substance of things hoped for, the evidence of things not seen."

HEB. 11:1

The very reason for the law of assumption is contained in this quotation. If there were not a deep seated awareness that that which you hope for had substance and was possible of attainment it would be impossible to assume the consciousness of being or having it. It is the fact that *creation is finished and everything exists that stirs you to hope*—and hope, in turn, *implies expectation*, and without expectation of success it would be impossible to use consciously the law of assumption. "Evidence" is a sign of actuality. Thus, this quotation means that *faith is the awareness of the reality of that which you assume*. Consequently, it is obvious that a lack of faith means disbelief in the existence of that which you desire. Inasmuch as that which you experience is the faithful reproduction of your state of consciousness, lack of faith will mean perpetual failure in any *conscious* use of the law of assumption.

In all the ages of history faith has played a major role. It permeates all the great religions of the world, it is woven all through mythology and yet, today, it is almost universally misunderstood.

Contrary to popular opinion, the efficacy of faith is not due to the work of any outside agency. It is from first to last *an activity of your own consciousness.*

The Bible is full of many statements about faith, the true meaning of which few are aware. Here are some typical examples:

> "Unto us was the gospel preached, as well as unto them: but the word preached did not profit them, not being mixed with faith in them that heard it."
>
> Heb. 4:2

In this quotation the 'us' and 'them' make clear that all of us hear the gospel. "Gospel" means good news. Very obviously good news for you would be that you had attained your desire. This is always being 'preached' to you by your infinite self. To hear that which you desire does exist and you need only to accept it in consciousness is good news.

Not "mixing with faith" means to deny the reality of that which you desire. Hence there is no "profit" (attainment) possible.

> "O faithless and perverse generation, how long shall I be with you."
>
> Matt. 17:17

The meaning of "faithless" has been made clear. "Perverse" means turned the wrong way, in other words, the consciousness of *not* being what you want to be. To be faithless, that is, to disbelieve in the reality of that which you assume, is to be perverse. "How long shall I be with you" means that the fulfillment of your desire is *predicated upon your change to the right state of consciousness.* It is just as though that which you desire is telling you that it will not be yours until you turn from being faithless and perverse to righteousness. As already stated, righteousness is the consciousness of already being what you want to be.

> "By faith he forsook Egypt, not fearing the wrath of the king: for he endured, as seeing him who is invisible."
>
> Heb. 11:27

"Egypt" means darkness, belief in many gods (causes). The "king" symbolizes the power of outside conditions or circumstances. "He" is your concept of yourself as already being what you want to be. "Enduring as seeing him who is invisible" means persisting in the assumption that your desire is *already* fulfilled. Thus this quotation means that by persisting in the assumption that you already are the person you want to be you rise above all doubt, fear and belief in the power of outside conditions or circumstances; and your world inevitably conforms to your assumption.

The dictionary definitions of faith:

> "the ascent of the mind or understanding to the truth" —
> "unwavering adherence to principle"

are so pertinent that they might well have been written with the law of assumption in mind.

Faith does not question—Faith knows.

Chapter Twenty-six
Destiny

Your destiny is that which you must inevitably experience. Really it is an infinite number of individual destinies, each of which when attained is the starting place for a new destiny.

Since life is *infinite* the concept of an ultimate destiny is inconceivable. When we understand that consciousness is the only reality, we know that it is the only creator. This means that your consciousness is the creator of your destiny. The fact is, you are creating your destiny every moment, *whether you know it or not.* Much that is good and even wonderful has come into your life without you having any inkling that you were the creator of it.

However, the understanding of the causes of your experience, and the *knowledge that you are the sole creator of the contents of your life, both good and bad, not only make you a much keener observer of all phenomena but through the awareness of the power of your own consciousness, intensifies your appreciation of the richness and grandeur of life.*

Regardless of occasional experiences to the contrary it is *your destiny to rise to higher and higher states of consciousness, and to bring into manifestation more and more of creation's infinite wonders.* Actually you are destined to reach the point where you realize that through your own desire you can consciously create your successive destinies.

The study of this book, with its detailed exposition of consciousness and the operation of the law of assumption, is the master key to the conscious attainment of your highest destiny.

This very day start your new life. Approach every experience in a new frame of mind—with a new state of consciousness. Assume the noblest and the best for yourself in every respect and continue therein.

Make believe—great wonders are possible.

Chapter Twenty-seven
Reverence

"Never wouldst Thou have made anything if Thou hadst not loved it."

WISDOM 11:24

In all creation, in all eternity, in all the realms of your infinite being the most wonderful fact is that which is stressed in the first chapter of this book. *You are God.* You are the "I am that I am." You are consciousness. You are the creator. This is the mystery, this is the great secret known by the seers, prophets and mystics throughout the ages. This is the truth that you can never know *intellectually.* Who is this you? That it is you, John Jones or Mary Smith is absurd. It is the *consciousness which knows* that you are John Jones or Mary Smith. It is your greater self, your deeper self, your infinite being. Call it what you will. The important thing is that *it is within you, it is you, it is your world.* It is this fact that underlies the immutable law of assumption. It is upon this fact that your very existence is built. It is this fact that is the foundation of every chapter of this book. No, you cannot know this intellectually, you cannot debate it, you cannot substantiate it. *You can only feel it. You can only be aware of it.*

Becoming aware of it, one great emotion permeates your being. You live with a perpetual feeling of *reverence*. The knowledge that your creator is the very self of yourself and never would have made you had he not *loved you* must fill your heart with devotion, yes, with adoration. One knowing glimpse of the world about you at any single instant of time is sufficient to fill you with profound awe and a feeling of worship.

It is when your feeling of reverence is most intense that you are closest to God and *when you are closest to God your life is richest.*

> "Our deepest feelings are precisely those we are least able to express, and even in the act of adoration, silence is our highest praise."

Awakened Imagination

To
Bill

Chapters

"Imagination, the real and eternal world of which this Vegetable Universe is but a faint shadow. What is the life of Man but Art and Science?"

William Blake, *"Jerusalem"*

"Imagination is more important than knowledge."

Albert Einstein, *on Science*

Chapter One
Who Is Your Imagination?

"I rest not from my great task
To open the Eternal Worlds, to open the immortal Eyes
Of Man inwards into the Worlds of Thought: into Eternity
Ever expanding in the Bosom of God, the Human
Imagination."

BLAKE: *"Jerusalem,"* 5:18-20

Certain words in the course of long use gather so many strange connotations that they almost cease to mean anything at all. Such a word is 'imagination.' This word is made to serve all manner of ideas, some of them directly opposed to one another. 'Fancy, thought, hallucination, suspicion:' indeed, so wide is its use and so varied its meanings, the word 'imagination' has no status nor fixed significance. For example, we ask a man to 'use his imagination,' meaning that his present outlook is too restricted and therefore not equal to the task. In the next breath we tell him that his ideas are 'pure imagination,' thereby implying that his ideas are unsound. We speak of a jealous or suspicious person as a 'victim of his own imagination,' meaning that his thoughts are untrue. A minute later we pay a man the highest tribute by describing him as a 'man of imagination.' Thus the word imagination has no definite meaning. Even the dictionary gives us no help. It defines imagination as (1) the picturing power or act of the mind, the constructive or creative principle; (2) a phantasm; (3) an irrational notion or belief; (4) planning, plotting or scheming as involving mental construction.

I identify the central figure of the Gospels with human imagination, the power which makes the forgiveness of sins, the achievement of our goals, inevitable.

> "All things were made by him; and without him was not anything made that was made."
>
> John 1:3

There is only one thing in the world, Imagination, and all our deformations of it.

> "He is despised and rejected of men; a man of sorrows, and acquainted with grief."
>
> Isaiah 53:3

Imagination is the very gateway of reality. "Man," said Blake, "is either the ark of God or a phantom of the earth and of the water." "Naturally he is only a natural organ subject to Sense." "The Eternal Body of Man is The Imagination: that is God himself, The Divine Body. י ש צ: Jesus: we are his Members."

I know of no greater and truer definition of the Imagination than that of Blake. By imagination we have the power to be anything we desire to be. Through imagination we disarm and transform the violence of the world. Our most intimate as well as our most casual relationships become imaginative as we awaken to "the mystery hid from the ages," that Christ in us is our imagination. We then realize that only as we live by imagination can we truly be said to live at all.

I want this book to be the simplest, clearest, frankest work I have the power to make it, that I may encourage you to function imaginatively, that you may open your "Immortal Eyes inwards into the Worlds of Thought," where you behold every desire of your heart as ripe grain "white already to harvest."

> "I am come that they might have life, and that they might have it more abundantly."
>
> John 10:10

The abundant life that Christ promised us is ours to experience *now,* but not until we have the sense of Christ *as our imagination* can we experience it.

> "The mystery hid from the ages . . . Christ in you, the hope of glory."
>
> Colossians 1:26

is your imagination. This is the mystery which I am ever striving to realize more keenly myself and to urge upon others.

Imagination is our redeemer, "the Lord from Heaven" born of man but not begotten of man.

Every man is Mary and birth to Christ must give. If the story of the immaculate conception and birth of Christ appears irrational to man, it is only because it is misread as biography, history and cosmology, and the modern explorers of the imagination do not help by calling It the unconscious or subconscious mind. Imagination's birth and growth is the gradual transition from a God of tradition to a God of experience. If the birth of Christ in man seems slow, it is only because man is unwilling to let go the comfortable but false anchorage of tradition.

When imagination is discovered as the first principle of religion, the stone of literal understanding will have felt the rod of Moses and, like the rock of Zin, issue forth the water of psychological meaning to quench the thirst of humanity; and all who take the proffered cup and live a life according to this truth, will transform the water of psychological meaning into the wine of forgiveness. Then, like the good Samaritan, they will pour it on the wounds of all.

The Son of God is not to be found in history nor in any external form. He can only be found as the imagination of him in whom His presence becomes manifest.

> "O would thy heart but be a manger for His birth! God would once more become a child on earth."

Man is the garden in which this only begotten Son of God sleeps. He awakens this Son by lifting his imagination up to heaven and clothing men in godlike stature. We must go on imagining better than the best we know.

Man in the moment of his awakening to the imaginative life must meet the test of Sonship.

> "Father, reveal Thy Son in me" and
> "It pleased God to reveal His Son in me."
>
> Galatians 1:16

The supreme test of Sonship is the forgiveness of sin. The test that your imagination is Christ Jesus, the Son of God, is your ability to forgive sin. Sin means missing one's mark in life, falling short of one's ideal, failing to achieve one's aim. Forgiveness means identification of man with his ideal or aim in life. This is the work of awakened imagination, the supreme work, for it tests man's ability to enter into and partake of the nature of his opposite.

"Let the weak man say, I am strong."

Joel 3:10

Reasonably this is impossible. Only awakened imagination can enter into and partake of the nature of its opposite.

This conception of Christ Jesus as human imagination raises these fundamental questions. Is imagination a power sufficient, not merely to enable me to assume that I am strong, but is it also of itself capable of executing the idea? Suppose that I desire to be in some other place or situation. Could I, by imagining myself into such a state and place, bring about their physical realization? Suppose I could not afford the journey and suppose my present social and financial status oppose the idea that I want to realize. Would imagination be sufficient of itself to incarnate these desires? Does imagination comprehend reason? By reason I mean deductions from the observations of the senses. Does it recognize the external world of facts? In the practical way of every-day life is imagination a complete guide to behaviour? Suppose I am capable of acting with continuous imagination, that is, suppose I am capable of sustaining the feeling of my wish fulfilled, will my assumption harden into fact? And, if it does harden into fact, shall I on reflection find that my actions through the period of incubation have been reasonable? Is my imagination a power sufficient, not merely to assume the feeling of the wish fulfilled, but is it also of itself capable of incarnating the idea? After assuming that I am already what I want to be, must I continually guide myself by reasonable ideas and actions in order to bring about the fulfillment of my assumption?

Experience has convinced me that an assumption, though false, if persisted in will harden into fact, that continuous imagination is sufficient for all things and all my reasonable plans and actions will never make up for my lack of continuous imagination.

Is it not true that the teachings of the Gospels can only be received in terms of faith and that the Son of God is constantly looking for signs of faith in people, that is, faith in their own imagination? Is not the promise

> "Believe that ye receive and ye shall receive."
>
> Mark 11:24

the same as "Imagine that you are and you shall be"? Was it not an imaginary state in which Moses

> "Endured, as seeing him who is invisible"?
>
> Hebrews 11:27

Was it not by the power of his own imagination that he endured?

Truth depends upon the intensity of the imagination not

upon external facts. Facts are the fruit bearing witness of the use or misuse of the imagination. Man becomes what he imagines. He has a self-determined history. Imagination is the way, the truth, the life revealed. We cannot get hold of truth with the logical mind. Where the natural man of sense sees a bud, imagination sees a rose full-blown. Truth cannot be encompassed by facts. As we awaken to the imaginative life we discover that to imagine a thing is so makes it so, that a true judgment need not conform to the external reality to which it relates.

The imaginative man does not deny the reality of the sensuous outer world of Becoming, but he knows that it is the inner world of continuous Imagination that is the force by which the sensuous outer world of Becoming is brought to pass. He sees the outer world and all its happenings as projections of the inner world of Imagination. To him everything is a manifestation of the mental activity which goes on in man's imagination without the sensuous reasonable man being aware of it. But he realizes that every man must become conscious of this inner activity and see the relationship between the inner causal world of imagination and the sensuous outer world of effects.

It is a marvelous thing to find that you can imagine yourself into the state of your fulfilled desire and escape from the jails which ignorance built.

The Real Man is a Magnificent Imagination.

It is this *self* that must be awakened.

> "Awake thou that sleepest, and arise from the dead, and Christ shall give thee light."
>
> Ephesians 5:14

The moment man discovers that his imagination is Christ he accomplishes acts which on this level can only be called miraculous. But until man has the sense of Christ *as his imagination*

> "You did not choose me, I have chosen you"
>
> John 15:16

he will see everything in pure objectivity without any subjective relationship. Not realizing that all that he encounters is part of himself, he rebels at the thought that he has chosen the conditions of his life, that they are related by affinity to his own mental activity. Man must firmly come to believe that reality lies within him and not without.

Although others have bodies, a life of their own, their reality is rooted in you, ends in you, as yours ends in God.

Chapter Two
Sealed Instructions

"The first power that meets us at the threshold of the soul's domain is the power of imagination."

Dr. Franz Hartmann

I was first made conscious of the power, nature and redemptive function of imagination through the teachings of my friend Abdullah; and through subsequent experiences I learned that Jesus was a symbol of the coming of imagination to man, that the test of His birth in man was the individual's ability to forgive sin; that is, his ability to identify himself or another with his aim in life.

Without the identification of man with his aim the forgiveness of sin is an impossibility, and only the Son of God can forgive sin. Therefore man's ability to identify himself with his aim, though reason and his senses deny it, is proof of the birth of Christ in him. To passively surrender to appearances and bow before the evidence of facts is to confess that Christ is not yet born in you.

Although this teaching shocked and repelled me at first,—for I was a convinced and earnest Christian, and did not then know that Christianity could not be inherited by the mere accident of birth but must be consciously adopted as a way of life,—it stole later on, through visions, mystical revelations and practical experiences, into my understanding and found its interpretation in a deeper mood. But I must confess that it is a trying time when those things are shaken which one has always taken for granted.

> "Seest thou these great buildings? There shall not be left one stone upon another that shall not be thrown down."
>
> Mark 13:2

Not one stone of literal understanding will be left after one drinks the water of psychological meaning. All that has been built up by natural religion is cast into the flames of mental fire. Yet, what better way is there to understand Christ Jesus than to identify the central character of the Gospels with human imagination—knowing that every time you exercise your imagination lovingly on behalf of another you are literally mediating God to man and thereby feeding and clothing Christ Jesus, and that whenever you imagine evil against another you are literally beating and crucifying Christ Jesus? Every imagination of man is either the cup of cold water or the sponge of vinegar to the parched lips of Christ.

> "Let none of you imagine evil in your hearts against his neighbor"

warned the prophet Zechariah. When man heeds this advice he will awake from the imposed sleep of Adam into the full consciousness of the Son of God. He is in the world and the world is made by him and the world knows him not: Human Imagination.

I asked myself many times "If my imagination is Christ Jesus and all things are possible to Christ Jesus, are all things possible to me?"

Through experience I have come to know that when I identify myself with my aim in life, then Christ is awake in me.

Christ is sufficient for all things.

> "I lay down my life that I might take it again. No man taketh it from me but I lay it down of myself."
>
> John 10:18

What a comfort it is to know that all that I experience is the result of my own standard of beliefs; that I am the center of my own web of circumstances and that as I change so must my outer world!

The world presents different appearances according as our states of consciousness differ. What we see when we are identified with a state cannot be seen when we are no longer fused with it. By state is meant all that man believes and consents to as true. No idea presented to the mind can realize itself unless the mind accepts it. It depends on the acceptance, the state with which we are identified, how things present themselves. In the fusion of imagination and states is to be found the shaping of the world as it seems. The world is a revelation of the states with which imagination is fused. It is the state *from* which we think that determines the objective world in which we live. The rich man, the poor man, the good man, the thief, are what they are by virtue of the states *from* which they view the world. On the distinction between these states depends the distinction between the worlds of these men. Individually so different is this same world. It is not the actions and behavior of the good man that should be matched but his point of view. Outer reforms are useless if the inner state is not changed. Success is gained not by imitating the outer actions of the successful but by right inner actions and inner talking.

If we detach ourselves from a state, and we may at any moment, the conditions and circumstances to which that union gave being vanish.

It was in the fall of 1933 in New York City that I approached Abdullah with a problem. He asked me one simple question, "What do you want?" I told him that I would like to spend the winter in Barbados, but that I was broke. I literally did not have a nickel.

"If you will imagine yourself to be *in* Barbados," said he, "thinking and viewing the world *from* that state of consciousness instead of thinking *of* Barbados, you will spend the winter there. You must not concern yourself with the ways and means of getting there, for the state of consciousness of already being in Barbados, if occupied by your imagination, will devise the means best suited to realize itself."

Man lives by committing himself to invisible states, by fusing his imagination with what he knows to be other than himself, and in this union he experiences the results of that fusion. No one can lose what he has save by detachment from the state where the things experienced have their natural life.

"You must imagine yourself right into the state of your fulfilled desire," Abdullah told me, "and fall asleep viewing the world from Barbados."

The world which we describe from observation must be as we describe it relative to ourselves. Our imagination connects us with the state desired. But we must use imagination masterfully, not as an onlooker thinking *of* the end, but as a partaker thinking *from* the end. We must actually *be* there in imagination. If we do this, our subjective experience will be realized objectively.

"This is not mere fancy," said he, "but a truth you can prove by experience."

His appeal to enter *into* the wish fulfilled was the secret of thinking *from* the end. Every state is already there as "mere possibility" as long as you think *of* it, but is overpoweringly real when you think *from* it. Thinking from the end is the way of Christ.

I began right there and then fixing my thoughts beyond the limits of sense, beyond that aspect to which my present state gave being, towards the feeling of already being *in* Barbados and viewing the world *from* that standpoint.

He emphasized the importance of the state *from* which man views the world as he falls asleep. All prophets claim that the voice of God is chiefly heard by man in dreams.

> "In a dream, in a vision of the night, when deep sleep falleth upon men, in slumberings upon the bed; then he openeth the ears of men, and sealeth their instruction."
>
> Job 33:15:16

That night and for several nights thereafter I fell asleep in the assumption that I was in my father's house in Barbados. Within a month I received a letter from my brother saying that he had a strong desire to have the family together at Christmas and asking me to use the enclosed steamship ticket for Barbados. I sailed two days after I received my brother's letter and spent a wonderful winter in Barbados.

This experience has convinced me that man can be anything he pleases if he will make the conception habitual and think *from* the end. It has also shown me that I can no longer excuse myself by placing the blame on the world of external things—that my good and my evil have no dependency except from myself—that it depends on the state *from* which I view the world how things present themselves.

Man who is free in his choice acts from conceptions which he freely, though not always wisely, chooses. All conceivable states are awaiting our choice and occupancy, but no amount of rationalizing will of itself yield us the state of consciousness which is the only thing worth having.

The imaginative image is the only thing to seek.

The ultimate purpose of imagination is to create in us "the spirit of Jesus," which is continual forgiveness of sin, continual identification of man with his ideal. Only by identifying ourselves with our aim can we forgive ourselves for having missed it. All else is labor in vain. On this path, to whatever place or state we convey our imagination to that place or state we will gravitate physically also.

> "In my Father's house are many mansions; if it were not so, I would have told you. I go to prepare a place for you. And if I go and prepare a place for you, I will come again, and receive you unto myself; that where I am there ye may be also."
>
> John 14:2

By sleeping in my father's house in my imagination as though I slept there in the flesh, I fused my imagination with that state and was compelled to experience that state in the flesh also.

So vivid was this state to me I could have been seen in my father's house had any sensitive entered the room where in imagination I was sleeping. A man can be seen where in imagination he is, for a man must be where his imagination is, for his imagination is himself. This I know from experience for I have been seen by a few to whom I desired to be seen, when physically I was hundreds of miles away.

I, by the intensity of my imagination and feeling, imagining and feeling myself to be *in* Barbados instead of merely thinking *of* Barbados, had spanned the vast Atlantic to influence my brother into desiring my presence to complete the family circle at Christmas. Thinking *from* the end, from the feeling of my wish fulfilled, was the source of everything that happened as outer cause, such as my brother's impulse to send me a steamship ticket; and it was also the cause of everything that appeared as results.

In "Ideas of Good and Evil" (Page 35) W. B. Yeats having described a few experiences similar to this experience of mine writes:

> "If all who have described events like this have not dreamed, we should rewrite our histories, for all men, certainly all imaginative men, must be forever casting forth enchantments, glamour, illusions; and all men, especially tranquil

> men who have no powerful egotistic life, must be continually passing under their power."

Determined imagination, thinking *from* the end, is the beginning of all miracles.

I would like to give you an immense belief in miracles, but a miracle is only the name given by those who have no knowledge of the power and function of imagination to the works of imagination. Imagining oneself into the feeling of the wish fulfilled is the means by which a new state is entered. This gives the state the quality of is-ness. Hermes tells us:

> "That which *is,* is manifested; that which has been or shall be, is unmanifested, but not dead; for Soul, the eternal activity of God, animates all things."

The future must become the present in the imagination of the one who would wisely and consciously create circumstances. We must translate vision into Being, thinking *of* into thinking *from*. Imagination must center itself in some state and view the world *from* that state. Thinking *from* the end is an intense perception of the world of fulfilled desire. Thinking *from* the state desired is creative living. Ignorance of this ability to think *from* the end is bondage. It is the root of all bondage with which man is bound. To passively surrender to the evidence of the senses under-estimates the capacities of the Inner Self. Once man accepts thinking *from* the end as a creative principle in which he can cooperate, then he is redeemed from the absurdity of ever attempting to achieve his objective by merely thinking *of* it.

Construct all ends according to the pattern of fulfilled desire.

The whole of life is just the appeasement of hunger, and the infinite states of consciousness from which a man can view the world are purely a means of satisfying that hunger. The principle upon which each state is organized is some form of hunger to lift the passion for self-gratification to ever higher and higher levels of experience. Desire is the mainspring of the mental machinery. It is a blessed thing. It is a right and natural craving which has a state of consciousness as its right and natural satisfaction.

> "But one thing I do, forgetting the things which are behind, and stretching forward to the things which are before, I press on toward the goal."
>
> Philippians 3:13

It is necessary to have an aim in life. Without an aim we drift. "What wantest thou of me?" is the implied question asked most often by the central figure of the Gospels. In defining your aim you must want it.

"As the hart panteth after the water brooks, so panteth my soul after thee, O God."

Psalms 42:1

It is lack of this passionate direction to life that makes man fail of accomplishment.

The spanning of the bridge between desire—thinking *of*—and satisfaction—thinking *from*—is all-important. We must move mentally from thinking *of* the end to thinking *from* the end. This, reason could never do. By its nature it is restricted to the evidence of the senses; but imagination, having no such limitation, can. Desire exists to be gratified in the activity of imagination. Through imagination man escapes from the limitation of the senses and the bondage of reason.

There is no stopping the man who can think *from* the end. Nothing can stop him. He creates the means and grows his way out of limitation into ever greater and greater mansions of the Lord. It does not matter what he has been or what he is. All that matters is 'what does he want'? He knows that the world is a manifestation of the mental activity which goes on within himself, so he strives to determine and control the ends *from* which he thinks. In his imagination he dwells in the end, confident that he shall dwell there in the flesh also. He puts his whole trust in the feeling of the wish fulfilled and lives by committing himself to that state, for the art of fortune is to tempt him so to do. Like the man at the pool of Bethesda, he is ready for the moving of the waters of imagination. Knowing that every desire is ripe grain to him who knows how to think *from* the end, he is indifferent to mere reasonable probability and confident that through continuous imagination his assumptions will harden into fact.

But how to persuade men everywhere that thinking *from* the end is the only living, how to foster it in every activity of man, how to reveal it as the plenitude of life and not the compensation of the disappointed: that is the problem.

Life is a controllable thing. You can experience what you please once you realize that you are His Son, and that you are what you are by virtue of the state of consciousness *from* which you think and view the world,

> "Son, thou art ever with me, and all that I have is thine."
>
> Luke 15:31

Chapter Three

Highways of the Inner World

"And the children struggled within her . . . and the Lord said unto her, two nations are in thy womb, and two manner of people shall be separated from thy bowels; and the one people shall be stronger than the other people; and the elder shall serve the younger."

GENESIS 25:22-23

Duality is an inherent condition of life. Everything that exists is double. Man is a dual creature with contrary principles embedded in his nature. They war within him and present attitudes to life which are antagonistic. This conflict is the eternal enterprise, the war in heaven, the never-ending struggle of the younger or inner man of imagination to assert His supremacy over the elder or outer man of sense.

"The first shall be last and the last shall be first."

Matthew 19:30

> "He it is, who coming after me is preferred before me."
>
> John 1:27

> "The second man is the Lord from heaven."
>
> I Cor. 15:47

Man begins to awake to the imaginative life the moment he feels the presence of another being in himself.

> "In your limbs lie nations twain, rival races from their birth; one the mastery shall gain, the younger o'er the elder reign."

There are two distinct centers of thought or outlooks on the world possessed by every man. The Bible speaks of these two outlooks as natural and spiritual.

> "The natural man receiveth not the things of the spirit of God: for they are foolishness unto him: neither can he know them, because they are spiritually discerned."
>
> I Corinthians 2:14

Man's inner body is as real in the world of subjective experience as his outer physical body is real in the world of external realities, but the inner body expresses a more fundamental part of reality. This existing inner body of man must be consciously exercised and directed. The inner world of thought and feeling to which the inner body is attuned has its real structure and exists in its own higher space.

There are two kinds of movement, one that is according to the inner body and another that is according to the outer body. The movement which is according to the inner body is causal, but the outer movement is under compulsion. The inner movement determines the outer which is joined to it, bringing into the outer a movement that is similar to the actions of the inner body. Inner movement is the force by which all events are brought to pass. Outer movement is subject to the compulsion applied to it by the movement of the inner body.

Whenever the actions of the inner body match the actions which the outer must take to appease desire, that desire will be realized.

Construct mentally a drama which implies that your desire is realized and make it one which involves movement of self. Immobilize your outer physical self. Act precisely as though you were going to take a nap, and start the predetermined action in imagination. A vivid representation of the action is the beginning of that action. Then, as you are falling asleep, consciously imagine yourself into the scene. The length of the sleep is not important, a short nap is sufficient, but carrying the action into sleep thickens fancy into fact.

At first your thoughts may be like rambling sheep that

have no shepherd. Don't despair. Should your attention stray seventy times seven, bring it back seventy times seven to its predetermined course until from sheer exhaustion it follows the appointed path. The inner journey must never be without direction. When you take to the inner road it is to do what you did mentally before you started. You go for the prize you have already seen and accepted.

In The Road to Xanadu (P. 103) Professor John Livingston Lowes says:

> "But I have long had the feeling, which this study has matured to a conviction, that Fancy and Imagination are not two powers at all, but one. The valid distinction which exists between them lies, not in the materials with which they operate, but in the degree of intensity of the operant power itself. Working at high tension the imaginative energy assimilates and transmutes; keyed low, the same energy aggregates and yokes together those images which at its highest pitch, it merges indissolubly into one."

Fancy assembles, imagination fuses.

Here is a practical application of this theory. A year ago a blind girl living in the city of San Francisco found herself confronted with a transportation problem. A rerouting of buses forced her to make three transfers between her home and her office. This lengthened her trip from fifteen minutes to two hours and fifteen minutes. She thought seriously about this problem and came to the decision that a car was the solution. She knew that she could not drive a car but felt that she could be driven in one. Putting this theory to the test that 'whenever the actions of the inner self correspond to the actions which the outer physical self must take to appease desire, that desire will be realized,' she said to herself "I will sit here and imagine that I am being driven to my office."

Sitting in her living room she began to imagine herself seated in a car. She felt the rhythm of the motor. She imagined that she smelled the odor of gasoline, felt the motion of the car, touched the sleeve of the driver and felt that the driver was a man. She felt the car stop, and turning to her companion, said "Thank you very much, sir." To which he replied, "The pleasure is all mine." Then she stepped from the car and heard the door snap shut as she closed it.

She told me that she centered her imagination on being *in* a car and although blind viewed the city from her imaginary ride. She did not think *of* the ride. She thought *from* the ride and all that *it* implied. This controlled and subjectively directed purposive ride raised her imagination to its full potency. She kept her purpose ever before her, knowing there was cohesion in purposive inner movement. In these mental journeys an emotional continuity must be sustained—the emotion of fulfilled desire. Expectancy and desire were so intensely joined that they passed at once from a mental state into a physical act.

The inner self moves along the predetermined course best when the emotions collaborate. The inner self must be fired, and it is best fired by the thought of great deeds and personal gain. We must take pleasure in our actions.

On two successive days the blind girl took her imaginary ride, giving it all the joy and sensory vividness of reality. A few hours after her second imaginary ride a friend told her of a story in the evening paper. It was a story of a man who was interested in the blind. The blind girl phoned him and stated her problem. The very next day, on his way home, he stopped in at a bar and while there had the urge to tell the story of the blind girl to his friend the proprietor. A total stranger, on hearing the story, volunteered to drive the blind girl home every day. The man who told the story then said, "If you will take her home, I will take her to work."

This was over a year ago, and since that day this blind girl has been driven to and from her office by these two gentlemen. Now, instead of spending two hours and fifteen minutes on three buses, she is at her office in less than fifteen minutes. And on that first ride to her office she turned to her good Samaritan and said, "Thank you very much, sir"; and he replied, "The pleasure is all mine."

Thus, the objects of her imagination were to her the realities of which the physical manifestation was only the witness. The determinative animating principle was the imaginative ride. Her triumph could be a surprise only to those who did not know of her inner ride. She mentally viewed the world from this imaginative ride with such a clearness of vision that every aspect of the city attained identity. These inner movements not only produce corresponding outer movements: this is the law which operates beneath all physical appearances. He who practices these exercises of bi-location will develop unusual powers of concentration and quiescence and will inevitably achieve waking consciousness on the inner and dimensionally larger world. Actualizing strongly she fulfilled her desire, for viewing the city *from* the feeling of her wish fulfilled, she matched the state desired and granted that to herself which sleeping men ask of God.

To realize your desire an action must start in your imagination, apart from the evidence of the senses, involving movement of self and implying fulfillment of your desire. Whenever it is the action which the outer self takes to appease desire, that desire will be realized.

The movement of every visible object is caused not by things outside the body but by things within it which operate from within outward. The journey is in yourself. You travel along the highways of the inner world. Without inner movement it is impossible to bring forth anything. Inner action is introverted sensation. If you will construct mentally a drama which implies that you have realized your objective, then close your eyes and drop your thoughts inward, centering your imagination all the while in the predetermined action and partake in that action, you will become a self-determined being.

Inner action orders all things according to the nature of itself. Try it and see whether a desirable ideal once formulated is possible, for only by this process of experiment can you realize your potentialities. It is thus that this creative principle is being realized. So the clue to purposive living is to center your imagination in the action and feeling of fulfilled desire with such awareness, such sensitiveness, that you initiate and experience movement upon the inner world.

Ideas only act if they are felt, if they awaken inner movement. Inner movement is conditioned by self-motivation, outer movement by compulsion.

> "Wherever the sole of your foot shall tread, the same give I unto you."
>
> Joshua 1:3

and remember

> "The Lord thy God in the midst of thee is mighty."
>
> Zephaniah 3:17

Chapter Four
The Pruning Shears of Revision

"The second man is the Lord from heaven"

I Corinthians 15:47

Never will he say caterpillars. He'll say, 'There's a lot of butterflies —as—is—to—be on our cabbages, Prue.' He won't say 'It's winter.' He'll say, 'Summer's sleeping.' And there's no bud little enough nor sad-coloured enough for Kester not to callen it the beginnings of the blow."

Mary Webb. (Precious Bane)

The very first act of correction or cure is always 'revise.' One must start with oneself. It is one's attitude that must be changed.

"What we are, that only can we see."

Emerson

It is a most healthy and productive exercise to daily relive the day as you wish you had lived it, revising the scenes to make them conform to your ideals. For instance, suppose today's mail brought disappointing news. Revise the letter. Mentally rewrite it and make it conform to the news you wish you had received. Then, in imagination, read the revised letter over and over again. This is the essence of revision and revision results in repeal.

The one requisite is to arouse your attention in a way and to such intensity that you become wholly absorbed in the revised action. You will experience an expansion and refinement of the senses by this imaginative exercise and eventually achieve vision. But always remember that the ultimate purpose of this exercise is to create in you "the Spirit of Jesus" which is continual forgiveness of sin.

Revision is of greatest importance when the motive is to change oneself, when there is a sincere desire to be something different, when the longing is to awaken the ideal active spirit of forgiveness. Without imagination man remains a being of sin. Man either goes forward to imagination or remains imprisoned in his senses. To go forward to imagination is to forgive. Forgiveness is the life of the imagination. The art of living is the art of forgiving. Forgiveness is, in fact, experiencing in imagination the revised version of the day, experiencing in imagination what you wish you had experienced in the flesh. Every time one really forgives; that is, every time one relives the event as it should have been lived, one is born again.

"Father forgive them" is not the plea that comes once a

year but the opportunity that comes every day. The idea of forgiving is a daily possibility, and, if it is sincerely done, it will lift man to higher and higher levels of being. He will experience a daily Easter and Easter is the idea of rising transformed. And that should be almost a continuous process.

Freedom and forgiveness are indissolubly linked. Not to forgive is to be at war with ourselves for we are freed according to our capacity to forgive.

> "Forgive, and you shall be forgiven."
>
> Luke 6:37

Forgive, not merely from a sense of duty or service, forgive because you want to.

> "Thy ways are ways of pleasantness and all thy paths are peace."
>
> Proverbs 3:17

You must take pleasure in revision. You can forgive others effectively only when you have a sincere desire to identify them with their ideal. Duty has no momentum. Forgiveness is a matter of deliberately withdrawing attention from the unrevised day and giving it full strength and joyously to the revised day. If a man begins to revise even a little of the vexations and troubles of the day, then he begins to work practically on himself. Every revision is a victory over himself and therefore a victory over his enemy.

> "A man's foes are those of his own household."
>
> Matthew 10:36

and his household is his state of mind. He changes his future as he revises his day.

When man practices the art of forgiveness, of revision, however factual the scene on which sight then rests, he revises it with his imagination and gazes on one never before witnessed. The magnitude of the change which any act of revision involves makes such change appear wholly improbable to the realist—the unimaginative man; but the radical changes in the fortunes of the Prodigal were all produced by a 'change of heart.'

The battle man fights is fought out *in his own imagination*. The man who does not revise the day has lost the vision of that life, into the likeness of which, it is the true labour of the 'Spirit of Jesus' to transform this life.

> "All things whatsoever ye would that men should do to you, even so do ye to them: for this is the law."
>
> Matthew 7:12

Here is the way an artist friend forgave herself and was set free from pain, annoyance and unfriendliness. Knowing that nothing but forgetfulness and forgiveness will bring us to new values, she cast herself upon her imagination and escaped from the prison of her senses. She writes:

"Thursday I taught all day in the art school. Only one small thing marred the day. Coming into my afternoon classroom I discovered the janitor had left all the chairs on top of the desks after cleaning the floor. As I lifted a chair down it slipped from my grasp and struck me a sharp blow on the instep of my right foot. I immediately examined my thoughts and found that I had criticized the man for not doing his job properly. Since he had lost his helper I realized he probably felt he had done more than enough and it was an unwanted gift that had bounced and hit me on the foot. Looking down at my foot I saw both my skin and nylons were intact so forgot the whole thing.

"That night, after I had been working intensely for about three hours on a drawing, I decided to make myself a cup of coffee. To my utter amazement I couldn't manage my right foot at all and it was giving out great bumps of pain. I hopped over to a chair and took off my slipper to look at it. The entire foot was a strange purplish pink, swollen out of shape and red hot. I tried walking on it and found that it just flapped. I had no control over it whatsoever. It looked like one of two things: either I had cracked a bone when I dropped the chair on it or something could be dislocated.

"'No use speculating what it is. Better get rid of it right

away.' So I became quiet all ready to melt myself into light. To my complete bewilderment my imagination refused to cooperate. It just said 'No.' This sort of thing often happens when I am painting. I just started to argue 'Why not?' It just kept saying 'No.' Finally I gave up and said 'You know I am in pain. I am trying hard not to be frightened, but you are the boss. What do you want to do?' The answer: 'Go to bed and review the day's events.' So I said 'All right. But let me tell you if my foot isn't perfect by tomorrow morning you have only yourself to blame.'

"After arranging the bed clothes so they didn't touch my foot I started to review the day. It was slow going as I had difficulty keeping my attention away from my foot. I went through the whole day, saw nothing to add to the chair incident. But when I reached the early evening I found myself coming face to face with a man who for the past year has made a point of not speaking. The first time this happened I thought he had grown deaf. I had known him since school days, but we had never done more than say 'hello' and comment on the weather. Mutual friends assured me I had done nothing, that he had said he never liked me and finally decided it was not worthwhile speaking. I had said 'Hi!' He hadn't answered. I found that I thought 'Poor guy—what a horrid state to be in. I shall do something about this ridiculous state of affairs,' So, in my imagination, I stopped right there and re-did the scene. I said 'Hi!' He answered 'Hi!'

and smiled. I now thought 'Good old Ed.' I ran the scene over a couple of times and went on to the next incident and finished up the day.

"'Now what—do we do my foot or the concert?' I had been melting and wrapping up a wonderful present of courage and success for a friend who was to make her debut the following day and I had been looking forward to giving it to her tonight. My imagination sounded a little bit solemn as it said 'Let us do the concert. It will be more fun.' 'But first couldn't we just take my perfectly good imagination foot out of this physical one before we start?' I pleaded. 'By all means.'

"That done, I had a lovely time at the concert and my friend got a tremendous ovation.

"By now I was very, very sleepy and fell asleep doing my project. The next morning, as I was putting on my slipper, I suddenly had a quick memory picture of withdrawing a discolored and swollen foot from the same slipper. I took my foot out and looked at it. It was perfectly normal in every respect. There was a tiny pink spot on the instep where I remembered I had hit it with the chair. 'What a vivid dream that was!' I thought and dressed. While waiting for my coffee I wandered over to my drafting table and saw that all my brushes were lying helter-skelter and unwashed. 'Whatever possessed you to leave your brushes like that?' 'Don't you remember? It was because of your foot.' So it hadn't been a dream after all but a beautiful healing."

She had won by the art of revision what she would never have won by force.

> "In Heaven the only Art of Living Is Forgetting & Forgiving Especially to the Female."
>
> Blake

We should take our life, not as it appears to be, but from the vision of this artist, from the vision of the world made perfect that is buried under all minds—buried and waiting for us to revise the day.

> "We are led to believe a lie when we see with, not through the eye."
>
> Blake

A revision of the day, and what she held to be so stubbornly real was no longer so to her and, like a dream, had quietly faded away.

You can revise the day to please yourself and by experiencing in imagination the revised speech and actions not only modify the trend of your life story but turn all its discords into harmonies. The one who discovers the secret of revision cannot do otherwise than let himself be guided by love. Your effectiveness will increase with practice. Revision is the way by which right can find its appropriate might.

"Resist not evil" for all passionate conflicts result in an interchange of characteristics.

> "To him that knoweth to do good, and doeth it not, to him it is sin."
>
> James 4:17

To know the truth you must live the truth and to live the truth your inner actions must match the actions of your fulfilled desire. Expectancy and desire must become one. Your outer world is only actualized inner movement. Through ignorance of the law of revision those who take to warfare are perpetually defeated.

Only concepts that idealize depict the truth.

Your ideal of man is his truest self. It is because I firmly believe that whatever is most profoundly imaginative is, in reality, most directly practical that I ask you to live imaginatively and to think into and to personally appropriate the transcendent saying "Christ in you, the hope of glory."

Don't blame; only resolve. It is not man and the earth at their loveliest, but you practicing the art of revision make paradise. The evidence of this truth can lie only in your own experience of it. Try revising the day. It is to the pruning shears of revision that we owe our prime fruit.

Chapter Five

The Coin of Heaven

"Does a firm persuasion that a thing is so, make it so?" And the prophet replied "All poets believe that it does. And in ages of imagination this firm persuasion removed mountains: but many are not capable of a firm persuasion of anything."

WILLIAM BLAKE, "MARRIAGE OF HEAVEN AND HELL."

"Let every man be fully persuaded in his own mind."

ROMANS 14:5

Persuasion is an inner effort of intense attention. To listen attentively as though you heard is to evoke, to activate. By listening you can hear what you want to hear and persuade those beyond the range of the outer ear. Speak it inwardly in your imagination only. Make your inner conversation match your fulfilled desire. What you desire to hear without, you must hear within. Embrace the without within and become one who hears only that which implies the fulfillment of his desire, and all the external happenings in the world will become a bridge leading to the objective realization of your desire.

Your inner speech is perpetually written all around you in happenings. Learn to relate these happenings to your inner speech and you will become self-taught. By inner speech is meant those mental conversations which you carry on with yourself. They may be inaudible when you are awake because of the noise and distractions of the outer world of becoming, but they are quite audible in deep meditation and dream. But whether they be audible or inaudible, you are their author and fashion your world in their likeness.

> "There is a God in heaven," and heaven is within you, "that revealeth secrets, and maketh known to the king Nebuchadnezzar what shall be in the latter days. Thy dream, and the visions of thy head upon thy bed, are these."
>
> Daniel 2:28

Inner speech from premises of fulfilled desire is the way to create an intelligible world for yourself. Observe your inner speech for it is the cause of future action. Inner speech reveals the state of consciousness from which you view the world. Make your inner speech match your fulfilled desire, for your inner speech is manifested all around you in happenings.

> "If any man offend not in word, the same is a perfect man and able also to bridle the whole body. Behold we put bits in the horses' mouths, that they may obey us; and we turn about their whole body. Behold also the ships, which though they be so great, and are driven by fierce winds, yet are they turned about with a very small helm, whithersoever the governor listeth. Even so the tongue is a little member, and boasteth great things. Behold, how great a matter a little fire kindleth."
>
> James 3:2-5

The whole manifested world goes to show us what use we have made of the Word—Inner Speech. An uncritical observation of our inner talking will reveal to us the ideas from which we view the world. Inner talking mirrors our imagination and our imagination mirrors the state with which it is fused. If the state with which we are fused is the cause of the phenomenon of our life, then we are relieved of the burden of wondering what to do, for we have no alternative but to identify ourselves with our aim; and inasmuch as the state with which we are identified mirrors itself in our inner speech, then to change the state with which we are fused, we must first change our inner talking. It is our inner conversations which make tomorrow's facts.

> "Put off the former conversation, the old man, which is corrupt . . . and be renewed in the spirit of your

mind . . . put on the new man, which is created in righteousness."

Ephesians 4:22-24

"Our minds, like our stomachs, are whetted by change of food."

Quintillian.

Stop all of the old mechanical negative inner talking and start a new positive and constructive inner speech from premises of fulfilled desire. Inner talking is the beginning, the sowing of the seeds of future action. To determine the action, you must consciously initiate and control your inner talking. Construct a sentence which implies the fulfillment of your aim, such as "I have a large steady dependable income, consistent with integrity and mutual benefit," or "I am happily married." "I am wanted." "I am contributing to the good of the world," and repeat such a sentence over and over until you are inwardly affected by it. Our inner speech represents in various ways the world we live in.

"In the beginning was the Word,"

John 1:1

"That which ye sow ye reap. See yonder fields! The sesamum was sesamum, the corn was corn. The Silence and the Darkness Knew! So is a man's fate born."

The Light of Asia

Ends run true to origins.

"Those that go searching for love only make manifest their own lovelessness. And the loveless never find love, only the loving find love, and they never have to seek for it."

D. H. Lawrence

Man attracts what he *is*. The art of life is to sustain the feeling of the wish fulfilled and let things come to you, not to go after them or think they flee away.

Observe your inner talking and remember your aim. Do they match? Does your inner talking match what you would say audibly had you achieved your goal? The individual's inner speech and actions attract the conditions of his life. Through uncritical self-observation of your inner talking you find where you are in the inner world, and where you are in the inner world is what you are in the outer world. You put on the new man whenever ideals and inner speech match. In this way alone can the new man be born.

Inner talking matures in the dark. From the dark it issues into the light. The right inner speech is the speech that would be yours were you to realize your ideal. In other words, it is the speech of fulfilled desire.

"I am that."

"There are two gifts which God has bestowed upon man alone, and on no other mortal creature. These two are mind and speech; and the gift of mind and speech is equivalent to that of immortality. If a man uses these two gifts rightly, he will differ in nothing from the immortals . . . and when he quits the body, mind and speech will be his guides, and by them he will be brought into the troop of the gods and the souls that have attained to bliss."

Walter Scott's translation "Hermetica," Vol. 1, p. 231, Oxford University Press, 1924.

The circumstances and conditions of life are out-pictured inner talking, solidified sound. Inner speech calls events into existence. In every event is the creative sound that is its life and being. All that a man believes and consents to as true reveals itself in his inner speech. It is his Word, his life.

Try to notice what you are saying in yourself at this moment, to what thoughts and feelings you are consenting. They will be perfectly woven into your tapestry of life. To change your life you must change your inner talking for "life," said Hermes, "is the union of Word and Mind." When imagination matches your inner speech to fulfilled desire there will then be a straight path in yourself from within out, and the without will instantly reflect the within for you, and you will know reality is only actualized inner talking.

"Receive with meekness the inborn Word which is able to save your souls."

James 1:21

Every stage of man's progress is made by the conscious exercise of his imagination matching his inner speech to his fulfilled desire. Because man does not perfectly match them the results are uncertain while they might be perfectly certain. Persistent assumption of the wish fulfilled is the means of fulfilling the intention. As we control our inner talking, matching it to our fulfilled desires, we can lay aside all other processes. Then we simply act by clear imagination and intention. We imagine the wish fulfilled and carry on mental conversations from that premise.

Through controlled inner talking from premises of fulfilled desire seeming miracles are performed. The future becomes the present and reveals itself in our inner speech. To be held by the inner speech of fulfilled desire is to be safely anchored in life. Our lives may seem to be broken by events but they are never broken so long as we retain the inner speech of fulfilled desire. All happiness depends on the active voluntary use of imagination to construct and inwardly affirm that we are what we want to be. We match ourselves to our ideals by constantly remembering our aim and identifying ourselves with it. We fuse with our aims by frequently occupying the feeling of our wish fulfilled. It is the frequency, the habitual occupancy, that is the secret of success. The oftener we do it, the more natural it is. Fancy assembles. Continuous imagination fuses.

It is possible to resolve every situation by the proper use of imagination. Our task is to get the right sentence, the one which implies that our desire is realized and fire the imagination with it. All this is intimately connected with the mystery of "the still small voice."

Inner talking reveals the activities of imagination, activities which are the causes of the circumstances of life. As a rule man is totally unaware of his inner talking and therefore sees himself not as the cause but the victim of circumstance. To consciously create circumstance man must consciously direct his inner speech, matching "the still small voice" to his fulfilled desires.

> "He calls things not seen as though they were."
>
> Romans 4:17

Right inner speech is essential. It is the greatest of the arts. It is the way out of limitation into freedom. Ignorance of this art has made the world a battlefield and penitentiary where blood and sweat alone are expected, when it should be a place of marvelling and wondering. Right inner talking is the first step to becoming what you want to be.

> "Speech is an image of mind, and mind is an image of God."
>
> Hermetica, Vol. 1. P. 231

On the morning of April 12, 1953, my wife was awakened by the sound of a great voice of authority speaking within her and saying, "You must stop spending your thoughts, time and money. Everything in life must be an investment."

To spend is to waste, to squander, to lay out without return. To invest is to lay out for a purpose from which a profit is expected. This revelation of my wife is about the importance of the moment. It is about the transformation of the moment. What we desire does not lie in the future but in ourselves at this very moment. At any moment in our lives we are faced with an infinite choice: 'what we are and what we want to be.' And what we want to be is already existent, but to realize it we must match our inner speech and actions to it.

> "If two of you shall agree on earth as touching anything that they shall ask, it shall be done for them of my Father which is in heaven."
>
> Matthew 18:19

It is only what is done *now* that counts. The present moment does not recede into the past. It advances into the future to confront us, spent or invested. Thought is the coin of heaven. Money is its earthly symbol. Every moment must be invested and our inner talking reveals whether we are spending or investing. Be more interested in what you are inwardly 'saying now' than what you have 'said' by choosing wisely what you think and what you feel *now*.

Any time we feel misunderstood, misused, neglected, suspicious, afraid, we are spending our thoughts and wasting our time. Whenever we assume the feeling of being what we want to be, we are investing. We cannot abandon the moment to negative inner talking and expect to retain command of life. Before us goes the results of all that seemingly is behind. Not gone is the last moment—but oncoming.

> "My word shall not return unto me void, but it shall accomplish that which I please, and it shall prosper in the thing whereto I sent it."
>
> Isaiah 55:11

The circumstances of life are the muffled utterances of the inner talking that made them—the word made visible.

> "The Word," said Hermes, "is Son, and the Mind is Father of the Word. They are not separate one from the other; for life is the union of Word and Mind."

> "He willed us forth from Himself by the Word of truth."
>
> James 1:18

Let us

> "be imitators of God as dear children"
>
> Ephesians 5:1

and use our inner speech wisely to mould an outer world in harmony with our ideal.

> "The Lord spake by me, and his Word was in my tongue."
>
> 2 Samuel 23:2

The mouth of God is the mind of man. Feed God only the best.

> "Whatsoever things are of good report . . . think on these things."
>
> Philippians 4:8

The present moment is always precisely right for an investment, to inwardly speak the right word.

> "The word is very near to you, in your mouth, and in your heart, that you may do it. See, I have set before you this day life and good, death and evil, blessings and cursings, choose life."
>
> Deuteronomy 30:14-15

You choose life and good and blessings by *being* that which you choose. Like is known to like alone. Make your inner speech bless and give good reports. Man's ignorance of the future is the result of his ignorance of his inner talking. His inner talking mirrors his imagination and his imagination is a government in which the opposition never comes into power.

If the reader ask "What if the inner speech remains subjective and is unable to find an object for its love?" the answer is: it will not remain subjective, for the very simple reason that inner speech is always objectifying itself. What frustrates and festers and becomes the disease that afflicts humanity is man's ignorance of the art of matching inner words to fulfilled desire. Inner speech mirrors imagination and imagination is Christ.

Alter your inner speech, and your perceptual world changes. Whenever inner speech and desire are in conflict inner speech invariably wins. Because inner speech objectifies itself, it is easy to see that if it matches desire, desire will be objectively realized. Were this not so I would say with Blake

> "Sooner murder an infant in its cradle than nurse unacted desires."

But I know from experience

> "The tongue . . . setteth on fire the course of nature."
>
> James 3:6

Chapter Six

It Is Within

". . . Rivers, Mountains, Cities, Villages,
All are Human, & when you enter into their Bosoms
you walk
In Heavens & Earths, as in your own Bosom you bear your
Heaven
And Earth & all you behold; tho' it appears Without, it is
Within,
In your Imagination, of which this World of Mortality is
but a Shadow."

BLAKE: "JERUSALEM" P. 71, LINES 15-9

The inner world was as real to Blake as the outer land of waking life. He looked upon his dreams and visions as the realities of the forms of nature. Blake reduced everything to the bed-rock of his own consciousness.

"The Kingdom of Heaven is within you."

Luke 17:21

The Real Man, the Imaginative Man, has invested the outer world with all of its properties. The apparent reality of the outer world which is so hard to dissolve is only proof of the absolute reality of the inner world of his own imagination.

> "No man can come to me, except the Father which hath sent me draw him: . . . I and my Father are one."
>
> John 6:44
> John 10:30

The world which is described from observation is a manifestation of the mental activity of the observer. When man discovers that his world is his own mental activity made visible, that no man can come unto him except he draws him, and that there is no one to change but himself, his own imaginative self, his first impulse is to reshape the world in the image of his ideal. But his ideal is not so easily incarnated. In that moment when he ceases to conform to external discipline he must impose upon himself a far more rigorous discipline, the self-discipline upon which the realization of his ideal depends.

Imagination is not entirely untrammelled and free to move at will without any rules to constrain it. In fact, the contrary is true. Imagination travels according to habit. Imagination has choice, but it chooses according to habit. Awake or asleep, man's imagination is constrained to follow certain definite patterns. It is this benumbing influence of habit that man must change; if he does not, his dreams will fade under the paralysis of custom.

Imagination, which is Christ in man, is not subject to the necessity to produce only that which is perfect and good. It exercises its absolute freedom from necessity by endowing the outer physical self with free will to choose to follow good or evil, order or disorder.

> "Choose this day whom ye will serve."
>
> Joshua 24:15

But after the choice is made and accepted so that it forms the individual's habitual consciousness, then imagination manifests its infinite power and wisdom by moulding the outer sensuous world of becoming in the image of the habitual inner speech and actions of the individual.

To realize his ideal man must first change the pattern which his imagination has followed. Habitual thought is indicative of character. The way to change the outer world is to make the inner speech and action match the outer speech and action of fulfilled desire.

Our ideals are waiting to be incarnated but unless we ourselves match our inner speech and action to the speech and action of fulfilled desire, they are incapable of birth. Inner speech and action are the channels of God's action. He cannot respond to our prayer unless these paths are offered. The outer behavior of man is mechanical. It is subject to the compulsion applied to it by the behavior of the inner self, and old habits of the inner self hang on till replaced by new ones. It is a peculiar property of the second or inner man that he gives to the outer self something similar to his own reality of being. Any change in the behavior of the inner self will result in corresponding outer changes.

The mystic calls a change of consciousness 'death.' By death he means, not the destruction of imagination and the state with which it was fused, but the dissolution of their union. Fusion is union rather than oneness. Thus the conditions to which that union gave being vanish. "I die daily," said Paul to the Corinthians. Blake said to his friend Crabbe Robinson:

> "There is nothing like death. Death is the best thing that can happen in life; but most people die so late and take such an unmerciful time in dying. God knows, their neighbors never see them rise from the dead."

To the outer man of sense, who knows nothing of the inner man of Being, this is sheer nonsense. But Blake made the above quite clear when he wrote in the year before he died:

> "William Blake — one who is very much delighted with being in good company. Born 28 November 1757 in London and has died several times since."

When man has the sense of Christ *as his imagination,* he sees why Christ must die and rise again from the dead to save man—why he must detach his imagination from his present state and match it to a higher concept of himself if he would rise above his present limitations and thereby save himself.

Here is a lovely story of a mystical death which was witnessed by a 'neighbor.' "Last week," writes the one 'who rose from the dead,' "a friend offered me her home in the mountains for the Christmas holidays as she thought she might go east. She said that she would let me know this week. We had a very pleasant conversation and I mentioned you and your teaching in connection with a discussion of Dunne's 'Experiment With Time' which she had been reading.

"Her letter arrived Monday. As I picked it up I had a sudden sense of depression. However, when I read it she said I could have the house and told me where to get the keys. Instead of being cheerful I grew still more depressed, so much so I decided there must have been something between the lines which I was getting intuitively. I unfolded the letter and read the first page through and as I turned to the second page, I noticed she had written a postscript on the back of the first sheet. It consisted of an extremely blunt and heavy-handed description of an unlovely trait in my character which I had struggled for years to overcome and for the past two years I thought I had succeeded. Yet here it was again, described with clinical exactitude.

"I was stunned and desolated. I thought to myself, 'What is this letter trying to tell me? In the first place she invited me to use her house as I have been seeing myself in some lovely home during the holidays. In the second place, nothing comes to me except I draw it. And thirdly I have been hearing *nothing* but good news. So the obvious conclusion is that something in me corresponds to this letter and no matter what it looks like it is good news.'

"I reread the letter and as I did so I asked 'What is there here for me to see?' And then I saw. It started out 'After our conversation of last week I feel I can tell you . . .' and the rest of the page was as studded with 'weres' and 'wases' as currants in a seed cake. A great feeling of elation swept over me. It was *all* in the past. The thing I had labored so long to correct was *done*. I suddenly realized that my friend was a witness to my resurrection. I whirled around the studio chanting 'It's all in the past! It is done. Thank you, it is done!' I gathered all my gratitude up in a big ball of light and shot it straight to you and if you saw a flash of lightning Monday evening shortly after six your time, that was it.

"Now, instead of writing a polite letter because it is the correct thing to do, I can write giving sincere thanks for her frankness and thanking her for the loan of her house. Thank you so much for your teaching which has made my beloved imagination truly my Saviour."

And now, if any man shall say unto her

> "Lo, here is Christ, or there,"

she will believe it not, for she knows that the Kingdom of God is within her and that she herself must assume full responsibility for the incarnation of her ideal and that nothing but death and resurrection will bring her to it. She has found her Saviour, her beloved Imagination, forever expanding in the bosom of God.

There is only one reality, and that is Christ—Human Imagination, the inheritance and final achievement of the whole of Humanity

> "That we . . . speaking the truth in love, may grow up into him in all things, which is the head, even Christ."
>
> Ephesians 4:15

Chapter Seven
Creation Is Finished

"I am the beginning and the end, there is nothing to come that has not been, and is."

ECCLESIASTES 3:15 ERV

Blake saw all possible human situations as "already-made" *states.* He saw every aspect, every plot and drama as already worked out as 'mere possibilities' as long as we are not in them, but as overpowering realities when we are in them. He described these states as "Sculptures of Los's Halls."

> "Distinguish therefore states from Individuals in those States. States change but Individual Identities never change nor cease . . . The Imagination is not a State,"

Said Blake,

"It is the Human Existence itself. Affection or Love becomes a State when divided from Imagination."

Just how important this is to remember is almost impossible to say, but the moment the individual realizes this for the first time is the most momentous in his life, and to be encouraged to feel this is the highest form of encouragement it is possible to give.

This truth is common to all men, but the consciousness of it, and much more, the self-consciousness of it, is another matter.

The day I realized this great truth—that everything in my world is a manifestation of the mental activity which goes on within me, and that the conditions and circumstances of my life only reflect the state of consciousness with which I am fused—is the most momentous in my life. But the experience that brought me to this certainty is so remote from ordinary existence I have long hesitated to tell it, for my reason refused to admit the conclusions to which the experience impelled me. Nevertheless, this experience revealed to me that I am supreme within the circle of my own state of consciousness and that it is the state with which I am identified that determines what I experience. Therefore it should be shared with all, for to know this is to become free from the world's greatest tyranny, the belief in a second cause.

"Blessed are the pure in heart: for they shall see God."

Matthew 5:8

Blessed are they whose imagination has been so purged of the beliefs in second causes they know that imagination is all and all is imagination.

One day I quietly slipped from my apartment in New York City into some remote yesteryear's countryside. As I entered the dining room of a large inn I became fully conscious. I knew that my physical body was immobilized on my bed back in New York City. Yet here I was as awake and as conscious as I have ever been. I intuitively knew that if I could stop the activity of my mind everything before me would freeze. No sooner was the thought born than the urge to try it possessed me. I felt my head tighten, then thicken to a stillness. My attention concentrated into a crystal-clear focus and the waitress walking, walked not. And I looked through the window and the leaves falling, fell not. And the family of four eating, ate not. And they lifting the food, lifted it not. Then my attention relaxed, the tightness eased, and of a sudden all moved onward in their course. The leaves fell, the waitress walked and the family ate. Then I understood Blake's vision of the "Sculptures of Los's Halls."

"I sent you to reap that whereon ye bestowed no labor."

John 4:35

Creation is finished.

> "I am the beginning and the end, there is nothing to come that has not been, and is."
>
> Ecclesiastes 3:15, ERV

The world of creation is finished and its original is within us. We saw it before we set forth, and have since been trying to remember it and to activate sections of it. There are infinite views of it. Our task is to get the right view and by determined direction of our attention make it pass in procession before the inner eye. If we assemble the right sequence and experience it in imagination until it has the tone of reality, then we consciously create circumstances. This inner procession is the activity of imagination that must be consciously directed. We, by a series of mental transformations, become aware of increasing portions of that which already is, and by matching our own mental activity to that portion of creation which we desire to experience we activate it, resurrect it and give it life.

This experience of mine not only shows the world as a manifestation of the mental activity of the individual observer, but it also reveals our course of time as jumps of attention between eternal moments. An infinite abyss separates any two moments of ours. We by the movements of our attention give life to the "Sculptures of Los's Halls."

Think of the world as containing an infinite number of

states of consciousness from which it could be viewed. Think of these states as rooms or mansions in the House of God, and like the rooms of any house they are fixed relative to one another. But think of yourself, the Real Self, the Imaginative You, as the living, moving occupant of God's House. Each room contains some of Los's Sculptures, with infinite plots and dramas and situations already worked out but not activated. They are activated as soon as Human Imagination enters and fuses with them. Each represents certain mental and emotional activities. To enter a state man must consent to the ideas and feelings which it represents. These states represent an infinite number of possible mental transformations which man can experience. To move into another state or mansion necessitates a change of beliefs. All that you could ever desire is already present and only waits to be matched by your beliefs. But it must be matched, for that is the necessary condition by which alone it can be activated and objectified. Matching the beliefs of a state is the seeking that finds, the knocking to which is opened, the asking that receives. Go in and possess the land.

The moment man matches the beliefs of any state he fuses with it and this union results in the activation and projection of its plots, plans, dramas and situations. It becomes the individual's home from which he views the world. It is his workshop, and, if he is observant, he will see outer reality shaping itself upon the model of his imagination.

It is for this purpose of training us in image-making that we were made subject to the limitations of the senses and clothed in bodies of flesh. It is the awakening of the imagination, the returning of His Son, that our Father waits for.

> "The creature was made subject to vanity not willingly but by reason of Him who subjected it."
>
> Romans 8:20

But the victory of the Son, the return of the prodigal, assures us that

> "the creature shall be delivered from the bondage of corruption into the glorious liberty of the Sons of God."
>
> Romans 8:21

We were subjected to this biological experience because no one can know of imagination who has not been subjected to the vanities and limitations of the flesh, who has not taken his share of Sonship and gone prodigal, who has not experimented and tasted this cup of experience; and confusion will continue until man awakes and a fundamentally imaginative view of life has been reestablished and acknowledged as basic.

> "I should preach . . . the unsearchable riches of Christ and make all men see what is the fellowship of the mystery,

which from the beginning of the world has been hid in God, who created all things by Jesus Christ."

Ephesians 3:9

Bear in mind that Christ in you is your imagination.

As the appearance of our world is determined by the particular state with which we are fused, so may we determine our fate as individuals by fusing our imaginations with ideals we seek to realize. On the distinction between our states of consciousness depends the distinction between the circumstances and conditions of our lives. Man who is free in his choice of state often cries out to be saved from the state of his choice.

"And ye shall cry out in that day because of your king which ye shall have chosen you; and the Lord will not hear you in that day. Nevertheless the people refused to obey the voice of Samuel; and they said, Nay; but we will have a king over us."

1 Samuel 8:18, 19

Choose wisely the state that you will serve. All states are lifeless until imagination fuses with them.

"All things when they are admitted are made manifest by the light: for everything that is made manifest is light."

Ephesians 5:13

and

> "Ye are the light of the world,"
>
> Matthew 5:14

by which those ideas to which you have consented are made manifest.

Hold fast to your ideal. Nothing can take it from you but your imagination. Don't think *of* your ideal, think *from* it. It is only the ideals *from* which you think that are ever realized.

> "Man lives not by bread alone, but by every word that proceeds out of the mouth of God."
>
> Matthew 4:4

and 'the mouth of God' is the mind of man.

Become a drinker and an eater of the ideals you wish to realize. Have a set definite aim or your mind will wander and wandering it eats every negative suggestion. If you live right mentally everything else will be right. By a change of mental diet you can alter the course of observed events. But unless there is a change of mental diet your personal history remains the same. You illuminate or darken your life by the ideas to which you consent. Nothing is more important to you than the ideas on which you feed. And you feed on the ideas *from* which you think. If you find the world unchanged it is a sure sign that you are wanting in fidelity to the new mental diet which you neglect in order to condemn your environment. You are in need of a new and sustained attitude. You can be anything you please if you will make the conception habitual, for any idea which excludes all others from the field of attention discharges in action. The ideas and moods to which you constantly return define the state with which you are fused. Therefore train yourself to occupy more frequently the feeling of your wish fulfilled. This is creative magic. It is the way to work toward fusion with the desired state.

If you would assume the feeling of your wish fulfilled more frequently you would be master of your fate, but unfortunately you shut out your assumption for all but the occasional hour. Practice making real to yourself the feeling of the wish fulfilled. After you have assumed the feeling of the wish fulfilled, do not close the experience as you would a book, but carry it around like a fragrant odor. Instead of being completely forgotten let it remain in the atmosphere communicating its influence automatically to your actions and reactions. A mood, often repeated, gains a momentum that is hard to break or check. So be careful of the feelings you entertain. Habitual moods reveal the state with which you are fused.

It is always possible to pass from thinking *of* the end you desire to realize, to thinking *from* the end. But the crucial matter is thinking *from* the end, for thinking *from* means unification or fusion with the idea: whereas in thinking *of* the end there is always subject and object—the thinking individual and the thing thought. You must imagine yourself into the state of your wish fulfilled, in your love for that state, and in so doing live and think *from* it and no more *of* it. You pass from thinking *of* to thinking *from* by centering your imagination in the feeling of the wish fulfilled.

Chapter Eight
The Apple of God's Eye

"What think ye of the Christ? Whose Son is He?"

MATTHEW 22:42

When this question is asked of you, let your answer be, "Christ is my imagination," and, though I

"See not yet all things put under him,"

Hebrews 2:8

yet I know that I am Mary from whom sooner or later He shall be born, and eventually

"Do all things through Christ."

The birth of Christ is the awakening of the inner or Second man. It is becoming conscious of the mental activity within oneself, which activity continues whether we are conscious of it or not.

The birth of Christ does not bring any person from a distance, or make anything to be that was not there before. It is the unveiling of the Son of God in man. The Lord "cometh in clouds" is the prophet's description of the pulsating rings of golden liquid light on the head of him in whom He awakes. The coming is from within and not from without, as Christ is *in* us.

This great mystery

"God was manifest in the flesh"

begins with Advent, and it is appropriate that the cleansing of the Temple

"Which temple ye are,"

1 Corinthians 3:17

stands in the forefront of the Christian mysteries.

"The Kingdom of Heaven is within you."

Luke 17:21

Advent is unveiling the mystery of your being. If you will practice the art of revision by a life lived according to the wise, imaginative use of your inner speech and inner actions, in confidence that by the conscious use of "the power that worketh in us," Christ will awake in you. If you will believe it, trust it, act upon it, Christ will awake in you. This is Advent.

> "Great is the mystery, God was manifest in the flesh."
>
> I Timothy 3:16

From Advent on

> "He that toucheth you toucheth the apple of God's eye."
>
> Zechariah 2:8

About the Author

Born to an English family in Barbados, **Neville Goddard** (1905–1972) moved to New York City at age seventeen to study theater. In 1932, he abandoned his work as a dancer and actor to fully devote himself to his career as a metaphysical writer and lecturer. Using the solitary pen name Neville, he became one of the twentieth century's most original and charismatic purveyors of the philosophy generally called New Thought. Neville wrote ten books and was a popular speaker on metaphysical themes from the late 1930s until his death. Possessed of a self-educated and eclectic intellect, Neville exerted an influence on a wide range of spiritual thinkers and writers, from Joseph Murphy to Carlos Castaneda. The impact of his ideas continues to be felt in some of today's best-selling works of practical spirituality.

TARCHER
PENGUIN

FIND YOURSELF IN TARCHER CORNERSTONE EDITIONS . . .

a powerful new line of keepsake trade paperbacks that highlight the foundational works of ancient and modern spiritual literature.

The Essential Marcus Aurelius

Newly translated and introduced by Jacob Needleman and John P. Piazza

A stunningly relevant and reliable translation of the thoughts and aphorisms of the Stoic philosopher and Roman emperor Marcus Aurelius.

January 2008 ISBN 978-1-58542-617-1

Tao Te Ching

The New Translation from *Tao Te Ching: The Definitive Edition*
Lao Tzu, translated by Jonathan Star

"It would be hard to find a fresh approach to a text that ranks only behind the Bible as the most widely translated book in the world, but Star achieves that goal."

—NAPRA REVIEW

January 2008 ISBN 978-1-58542-618-8

---

www.penguin.com

Accept This Gift

Selections from *A Course in Miracles*

Edited by Frances Vaughan, Ph.D., and Roger Walsh, M.D., Ph.D.

Foreword by Marianne Williamson

"An invaluable collection from one of the great sources of the perennial wisdom—a gold mine of psychological and spiritual insights."

—Ken Wilber

January 2008 ISBN 978-1-58542-619-5

The Kybalion

Three Initiates

Who wrote this mysterious guide to the principles of esoteric psychology and worldly success? History has kept readers guessing. . . . Experience for yourself the intriguing ideas of an underground classic.

May 2008 ISBN 978-1-58542-643-0

The Spiritual Emerson

Ralph Waldo Emerson, introduction by Jacob Needleman

This concise volume collects the core writings that have made Ralph Waldo Emerson a key source of insight for spiritual seekers of every faith—with an introduction by the bestselling philosopher Jacob Needleman.

July 2008 ISBN 978-1-58542-642-3